£6.50

FRANCIS FRITH'S
COUNTY
MEMORIES

CORNWALL
COUNTY MEMORIES

PETER STANIER was born in Liskeard and has written a number of books and papers on Cornish subjects, in particular mining and quarrying, as well as Francis Frith's 'Cornwall Living Memories', 'Victorian and Edwardian Cornwall', 'Churches of East Cornwall', 'St Austell', 'St Austell Bay' and 'Newquay to St Ives'. He now lives with his family in Shaftesbury, Dorset, where he is a lecturer and writer on archaeology, industrial archaeology and landscapes.

POLPERRO, THE HARBOUR 1924 76331

FRANCIS FRITH'S
COUNTY
MEMORIES

CORNWALL
COUNTY MEMORIES

PETER STANIER

First published in hardback in 2003 as Photographic Memories of Britain - Cornwall
Revised and extended paperback edition published in the United Kingdom in 2006 by
The Francis Frith Collection as Cornwall, County Memories
Paperback Edition ISBN 1-84589-113-9

British Library Cataloguing in Publication Data

Cornwall County Memories
Peter Stanier

The Francis Frith Collection®
Frith's Barn, Teffont,
Salisbury, Wiltshire SP3 5QP
Tel: +44 (0) 1722 716 376
Email: info@francisfrith.co.uk
www.francisfrith.com

Aerial photographs reproduced under licence from Simmons Aerofilms Limited
Historical Ordnance Survey maps reproduced under licence from Homecheck.co.uk

Printed and bound in England

Front Cover: **ST COLUMB MAJOR, FORE STREET 1906** 56244t
The colour-tinting in this image is for illustrative purposes only,
and is not intended to be historically accurate

Every attempt has been made to contact copyright holders of illustrative material.
We will be happy to give full acknowledgement in future editions for any items not credited.
Any information should be directed to The Francis Frith Collection.

AS WITH ANY HISTORICAL DATABASE, THE FRANCIS FRITH ARCHIVE IS CONSTANTLY
BEING CORRECTED AND IMPROVED, AND THE PUBLISHERS WOULD WELCOME
INFORMATION ON OMISSIONS OR INACCURACIES

FRANCIS FRITH'S
COUNTY MEMORIES

CONTENTS

THE MAKING OF AN ARCHIVE

FRANCIS FRITH, Victorian founder of the world-famous photographic archive, was a devout Quaker and a highly successful Victorian businessman. By 1860 he was already a multi-millionaire, having established and sold a wholesale grocery business in Liverpool. He had also made a series of pioneering photographic journeys to the Nile region. The images he returned with were the talk of London. An eminent modern historian has likened their impact on the population of the time to that on our own generation of the first photographs taken on the surface of the moon.

Frith had a passion for landscape, and was as equally inspired by the countryside of Britain as he was by the desert regions of the Nile. He resolved to set out on a new career and to use his skills with a camera. He established a business in Reigate as a specialist publisher of topographical photographs.

Frith lived in an era of immense and sometimes violent change. For the poor in the early part of Victoria's reign work was a drudge and the hours long, and ordinary people had precious little free time. Most had not travelled far beyond the boundaries of their own town or village. Mass tourism was in its infancy during the 1860s, but during the next decade the railway network and the establishment of Bank Holidays and half-Saturdays gradually made it possible for the working man and his family to enjoy holidays and to see a little more of the world. With characteristic business acumen, Francis Frith foresaw that these new tourists would enjoy having souvenirs to commemorate their days out. He began selling photo-souvenirs of seaside resorts and beauty spots, which the Victorian public pasted into treasured family albums.

Frith's aim was to photograph every town and village in Britain. For the next thirty years he travelled the country by train and by pony and trap, producing fine photographs of seaside resorts and beauty spots that were keenly bought by millions of Victorians.

THE RISE OF FRITH & CO

Each photograph was taken with tourism in mind, the small team of Frith photographers concentrating on busy shopping streets, beaches, seafronts, picturesque lanes and villages. They also photographed buildings: the Victorian and Edwardian eras were times of huge building activity, and town halls, libraries, post offices, schools and technical colleges were springing up all over the country. They were invariably celebrated by a proud Victorian public, and photo souvenirs – visual records – published by F Frith & Co were sold in their hundreds of thousands. In addition, many new commercial buildings such as hotels, inns and pubs were photographed, often because their owners specifically commissioned Frith postcards or prints of them for re-sale or for publicity purposes.

In order to gain some understanding of the scale of Frith's business one only has to look at the catalogue issued by Frith & Co in 1886: it runs to some 670 pages. By 1890 Frith had created the greatest specialist photographic publishing company in the world, with over 2,000 stockists! The picture on the right shows the Frith & Co display board on the wall of the stockist at Ingleton in the Yorkshire Dales (left of window). Beautifully constructed with a mahogany frame and gilt inserts, it displayed a dozen scenes.

POSTCARD BONANZA

The ever-popular holiday postcard we know today took many years to appear, and F Frith & Co was in the vanguard of its development. Postcards became a hugely popular means of communication and sold in their millions. Frith's company took full advantage of this boom and soon became the major publisher of photographic view postcards.

Francis Frith died in 1898 at his villa in Cannes, his great project still growing. His sons Eustace and Cyril continued their father's monumental task, expanding the number of views offered to the public and recording more and more places in Britain, as the coasts and countryside were opened up to mass travel. The archive Frith created continued in business for another seventy years. By 1970 it contained over a third of a million pictures of 7,000 cities, towns and villages. The massive photographic record Frith has left to us stands as a living monument to a special and very remarkable man.

The archive's future is both bright and exciting. Francis Frith, with his unshakeable belief in making photographs available to the greatest number of people, would undoubtedly approve of what is being done today with his lifetime's work. His photographs depicting our shared past are now bringing pleasure and enlightenment to millions around the world a century and more after his death.

SCILLY ISLANDS

Round I.
White I.
St Helens
St Martins
Bryer
Gt Gauilly
Maidens
Bower
Tresco
Samson
St Mary's
Menfel
Hugh Town
Old Town
Annet
Geugh
St Agnes
Veladoua
Gorregan

BRISTOL CHA

Pentire
Trevose Head
PADSTO
Constantine
Bay
St Merryn
Little
St Ervan
St Eva
Watergate
Bay
Margan
St Columb Minor
Colan
Crantock
St Enode
Cubert
Newlyn
Ligan
or Perran
Bay
MIDSHALL OR
St MICHAEL
Peranzabuloe
St Allen
St Agnes
Agnes
Beacon
St Erme
Probu
Kenwyn
TRURO
Corne
Ilogan
St Clements
Merthe
REDRUTH
St Michael Penkevil
Leme
Railway
Kea
Gwithian
Gwennap
CAMBORNE
Verran Arworthal
Phillseigh
St Ives
Phillack
Stithians
cock
Cornminnis
Lelant
Carn
Chivias
St Just
Zennor
Towednack
Uny
Gwinear
Bonellis
St Jus
Gurnards Head
St Erth
PENRYN
Mylo
Morvah
Crowan
Mabe
MAWE
Madron
Ludgvan
St Hilary
Wendron
Budock
Nathon
St Just
Gulval
Germoe
Constantine
MARAZION
Breage
FALMOUTH
PENZANCE
Perran Uthnoe
Sithney
Mawnan
Sancreed
St Michael
Mount
HELSTON
Paul
Mount's
Bay
Mawgan
Helford
St Anthony in Meneage
White Sand
Bay
Burian
Manaccan
LANDS END
Sennen
St Martin
Dennis Point
St Levan
Gunwalloe
Cury
St Kevern
Tol Peden Penwith
Mullion
Ruan Major
Blackhead Point
Ruan Minor
Grade
Banks Head

VI°

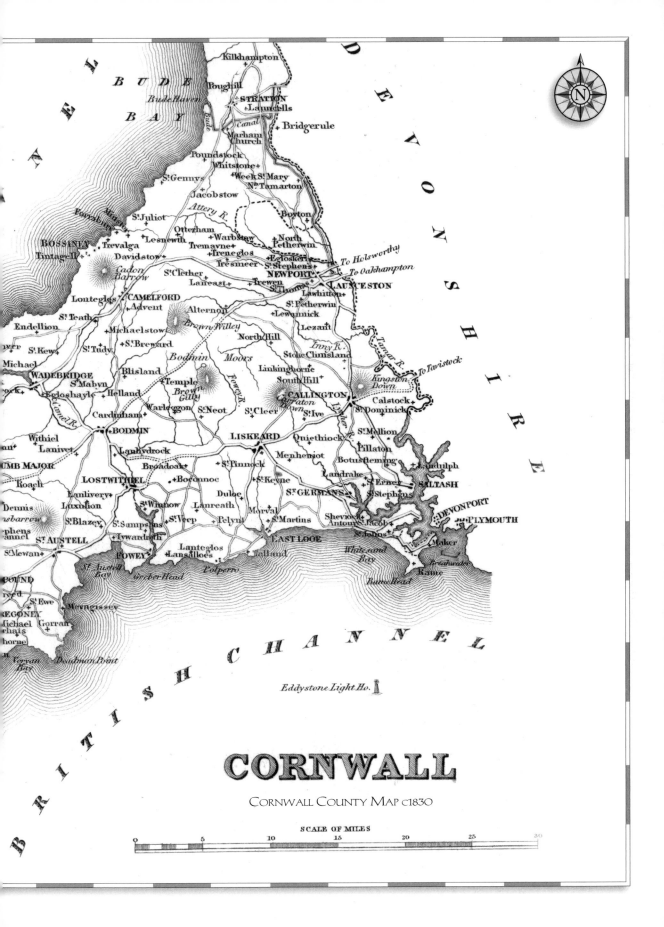

CORNWALL

CORNWALL COUNTY MAP c1830

SCALE OF MILES

0   5   10   15   20   25   30

INTRODUCTION

CORNWALL is special, and many will agree that this is one of the most distinctive and individual counties in all England. Cornwall shares its single border along the River Tamar with just one other county, Devon, which serves to emphasise its separateness in the far South West. Most routes into Cornwall pass over a Tamar crossing, each one giving a real sense of arrival for the visitor and a sense of coming home for every Cornish person. The most striking is perhaps the great suspension bridge across the Tamar at Saltash, alongside Brunel's railway bridge masterpiece, while downstream the slow moving Torpoint ferry gives enough time to contemplate the passage from one land into another. Gunnislake is another place with a genuine feel of a border crossing; all it lacks is a customs post at the end of the 500-year-old bridge that carries today's heavy traffic in from Tavistock. Motorists hardly notice the change, though, where the A30 sweeps in near Launceston, now by-passing the original bridge. The last major route is the A39, which follows the narrow watershed between the upper Tamar and the coast in the far north. There is almost a feel of creeping in by the back door until the first village of Kilkhampton is reached. Once across the border there are 80 miles of Cornwall before you, a long indented peninsula reaching out into the Atlantic, bounded on the south by the English Channel and on the north by the wilder approaches to the Bristol Channel. Ask any coastal walker, and they will tell you that the coastline is a challenging 270 miles of exceptional interest and beauty.

Nowhere in Cornwall is far from the sea or its influence, and the estuaries of the Tamar, Fowey, Fal, Helford and Camel bite far inland. They provided a valuable water highway in the past, but their hindering of land transport was only overcome by a ferry or bridge. Inlets and coves were a lifeline for trade and the once great fishing industry. Artificial harbours and breakwaters strengthened this reliance on the sea, as we can see at Falmouth, Par and Portreath.

ST MAWES, THE FRONT 1930 83179

While the sea has given up a rich harvest of fish, crabs, lobsters and even oysters in the estuaries, the hard granite rocks have yielded an unsurpassed mineral wealth - tin, copper, lead, zinc and other metals - hewn from deep mines at a great cost in lives and health. Alongside the mines, Cornwall is also famous for its quarries of granite, slate and china clay. On the high-hedged farms dairying and stock grazing have been important, and the mild climate, influenced by the surrounding sea, has allowed for crops of early potatoes and flowers, with broccoli too. There are areas of strange granite rocks and rugged cliffs, all in a windswept country with few trees, for the winter gales come straight in off the Atlantic. Woodland is only really seen in a few sheltered parts and deeper valleys.

Since Victorian times artists and photographers have found rich pickings in this varied landscape, so it is no surprise that Frith's men were here too. His photographers took hundreds of images from the late 19th century onwards, and the large collection contains a wealth of treasures to be tapped. In this selection there are views dating from the 1890s to the mid 1960s. This book includes some images of the same landscapes or towns which were photographed at different dates or angles, and are therefore well worth comparing for their changing details.

The photographs have been arranged by dividing Cornwall into four convenient parts. The Tamar and the East covers that block of land between the Tamar and Fowey estuaries, and starts with the dramatic railway viaduct at Calstock that was just nearing completion in 1907. The towns of Callington and Liskeard are represented, along with villages such as Dobwalls and Cheesewring. A journey along the coast takes in Downderry and Seaton, ending with the picturesque fishing ports of Looe and Polperro.

The stretch from Fowey to Falmouth is the central part of south Cornwall, reaching as far inland as Bodmin and including Lostwithiel, St Austell and Truro. The south coast is never far away, and there are scenes at Polkerris and Mevagissey, while commercial shipping is presented in the harbours of Fowey, Par and Falmouth.

The section on the Lizard and the Far West includes Cornwall's two largest and very distinct peninsulas. We begin just outside Falmouth on the north shore of the Helford River, a creek that almost cuts the Lizard peninsula off from the rest of Cornwall. The Lizard has the most southerly point in England, while Land's End is the most westerly and the most rugged landscape of all. Significant towns illustrated are Helston, Camborne, Redruth and Penzance, as well as St Ives and Hayle.

Finally, the chapter on the north coast takes in the rest of Cornwall from Hayle to Bude, and the remote Coombe valley in the farthest north. Along the way we see the bathing resorts of Newquay and Polzeath, along with striking coastal scenery.

Seafaring has always been part of the Cornish lifestyle. The little town of Fowey was important enough to have sent a fleet of 47 ships to the siege of Calais in 1346. We see a vista of its natural deep water harbour, with sailing ships waiting to load china clay. Just a few miles away is the artificial port of Par, enclosed by a breakwater but only accessible to small coasters, as it dries out at low tide. It spawned industries such as a granite works, lead smelter and flour mills, this last being a prominent landmark in the photograph. Ocean-going ships still call at the repair yard at Falmouth docks, seen in its early days in 1895. In contrast, there is the incredible little dock at Portreath, approached by a narrow entrance beneath fierce cliffs, which was once alive with sailing ships bringing Welsh coal and taking back copper ore for smelting. We see it in its last days when coal was still brought in by the occasional motor coaster. Pentewan on the south coast was another small dock – we see it as it was in 1912, with shipping in the distance. Bude, too, is shown with a few sailing ships that have entered the canal basin through the sea lock.

Images of the popular fishing ports of Looe, Polperro, Mevagissey, Padstow, Coverack and Cadgwith appear. The harbour at Mullion Cove was only 30 years old when it was photographed in 1924. It was built to encourage fishing and increase incomes in this area - there was only an open beach here before the harbour was built.

A superb picture of Pont Quay near Fowey encapsulates the whole theme of craft plying far inland to discharge valued cargoes for local communities. Today, that function is performed by lorries or even from the boot of a car after a visit to the supermarket. We also see the ancient ferry crossings on the estuaries. The King Harry chain ferry and the rowing boat at Malpas, both on the same river system, make a good contrast, while there are other ferries at Cremyll, Bodinnick, Percuil and Helford Passage. Lastly, lighthouses at St Anthony and Trevose Head were important aids to shipping.

Mining was such a large part of Cornish life, and is sadly not well represented in the photographs. However, we do see the Dolcoath Mine, once the greatest tin producer in Cornwall, which was sinking the new Williams' Shaft in 1902. This eventually went down over 3,000 feet. There is an equally dramatic view of the famous Delabole slate quarry, worked for centuries; by 1938 it was said to be approaching a depth of 500 feet and was the deepest in England.

Many settlements expanded in the 19th century in response to industrial activities, and this legacy is with us today: the cottages for miners and fishermen, and a remarkable number of non-conformist chapels. Towns like Camborne, Redruth, St Austell and the old market town of Liskeard all grew rich with mining and quarrying. We can study street scenes here and at Bodmin, Truro and Penzance. For a period a tram service linked the two towns of Camborne and Redruth, where in one photograph we have a glimpse of a tram.

Fishermen's houses are not forgotten in the narrow streets of St Ives or at Port Isaac, while there are also

DOWNDERRY, FROM THE SEASHORE 1930 83310

miners' villages at Cheesewring and St Day. Thatch appears in some villages, like Calenick, Feock and Cadgwith, while a thatcher is caught at work on a roof at Mawnan Smith. Prominent telephone poles and wires show that the 20th century had arrived in a number of villages such as Dobwalls and Mawnan Smith. Most village scenes of this period are traffic-free, but local inhabitants were stuck without a car and had to rely on an infrequent bus service or the services of delivery vans – we see one parked at Helford Passage.

Some individual houses are shown, and examples of hostelries are the Sloop Inn at St Ives, the Falcon Inn at St Mawgan and the Sportsman's Arms at Notter Bridge, along with purpose-built tourist hotels at Looe and Penzance; others appear incidentally in various town scenes.

Fowey has literary associations with Sir Arthur Quiller Couch, and the harbour view from Hall Walk was one of his favourites. We see two places where Daphne du Maurier lived: the house beside the water at Bodinnick, and Menabilly, the seat of the Rashleighs, one of the great Cornish families. Both locations were inspirations for her writing. Fowey also boasts Place House, home of the Treffrys. Another large house depicted in this selection is Lanhydrock near Bodmin, seat of the Robartes and now a National Trust property. It was photographed after a major rebuilding following a disastrous fire.

Cornwall has been transformed over the past 150 years by the growing tourist industry, which is now the main economic activity. Thousands of holidaymakers flock here every year seeking the beaches, picturesque seaside villages and harbours, or to walk in the landscape. While mass tourism is a phenomenon of the later 20th century, the idea is not new. Long before the Victorians, travellers ventured west into this remote land, and even John Wesley (who came with the higher purpose of preaching to Cornish working folk) ventured down to

the rocks at Land's End at the age of 82. Essential places to visit included Land's End, the Lizard or Bedruthan Steps, with perhaps a tin mine such as Botallack thrown in for good measure. The novelists Charles Dickens and Wilkie Collins both made tours of the county long before there was a main line railway from England. Tennyson later visited Land's End and stayed at a 'rackity, rather dirty inn' in 1860. The potential tourist market influenced the subject of photographs, as we see at Land's End with the First and Last House (and tree!), the most westerly post box, curious rocks and a souvenir seller.

The main line railway came to Cornwall in 1859 with the building of Isambard Kingdom Brunel's Saltash Bridge, and whole new opportunities were opened up. Passengers could reach Penzance within just a few hours of leaving Paddington in London, and once they had arrived, traps and other horse-drawn vehicles were on hand to take the visitor onwards. At St Austell, we see a bustling railway station, as well as an example of one of Brunel's timber 'fan' viaducts that were such a feature spanning the county's many valleys that had hitherto been an obstacle. In time, branch lines served other towns or growing resorts, such as Looe, Fowey, Newquay, Perranporth, Helston, Falmouth and St Ives. A second railway entered Cornwall at Launceston from Waterloo; here it dwindled to a single track as it wandered on to its far terminus at Padstow. A branch also ran to Bude, and there was the Calstock and Callington line too.

By the 1930s motoring holidays were becoming increasingly popular; trippers toured the countryside and reached places remote from the main highways and railways. Those were the carefree days when driving was a pleasure, before the roads to popular destinations became choked with traffic in summertime. In one photograph a car has even dared to venture into the narrow streets of Cadgwith. The railways, of course, could not compete against the door-to-door convenience of the motor car, and many lines were closed in the 1960s. Today, only the resorts of Looe, St Ives, Falmouth, Penzance and Newquay are served by railways.

The holiday industry was firmly established in the early 20th century, and it grew dramatically after the Second World War. Along the north coast there are photographs of holiday beaches at Hayle Towans, Perranporth, Newquay, Holywell Bay and Polzeath, all in their early years. Camping and caravanning holidays were coming to all parts of the county, and old-fashioned bell tents and early styles of caravans appear at Hayle Towans, Pentewan, Polzeath and Seaton. More traditional holiday centres are seen at Newquay and the promenade at Penzance.

Images of the prehistoric stone circles or ancient crosses at Quethiock and St Buryan, and the lost church at Penhale Sands are further reminders of Cornwall's rich heritage. Like Lanhydrock and other great houses, quaint ferry crossings, pretty fishing ports or the rugged scenic grandeur of Land's End or Kynance Cove, they are all invitations to go out and explore a unique county.

POLPERRO, THE HARBOUR 1924 76331

Above: CORNISH DELICACIES 1912 64860

Right: CHOOSE FER YERSELF 1923 73340

THE TAMAR AND THE EAST

Launceston is literally the gateway to Cornwall at the border with Devon. It boasts a Norman castle, a wealth of historic houses and a spacious square. The south gate with its twin arches is a remant of the walls which once enclosed Cornwall's only walled town.

LAUNCESTON, THE SQUARE 2003 L20701

This ancient town crowns the steep hill above the valley of the River Kensey. Here we see the broad market place, with its pleasing facades of 17th- and 18th-century slate-roofed buildings. In the centre there was once a circular Market Hall, where farmers and their wives gathered to buy and sell local produce. This has long since been demolished, and the area today is usually clogged by parked cars. The war memorial on the left is in the form of a market cross, and its foundation stone was laid in 1921 by the Prince of Wales.

THE TAMAR AND THE EAST

▼ CALSTOCK, THE VIADUCT 1907 59222

At this date the building of the new 12-arched viaduct across the Tamar is nearly finished, and the construction yard can be seen below on the Devon (right) bank. After opening in March 1908, the inhabitants of Calstock and the Callington area could travel by train direct to Plymouth. The tall chimney on the left is at the Calstock brick works.

◀ GUNNISLAKE
FORE STREET 2003 G68701

This long straggling village, in the centre of the old tin mining district, sits on a steep hill running down to the Tamar. We are at the bottom of Fore Street looking towards Newbridge Hill. An earlier Frith view from 1908 shows that the buildings have hardly changed, although the scene looks very different today. Where there was once a plain, dusty street there is now tarmac, with pavements built out into the road for traffic-calming. On the extreme left is the Buccaneer, once Bond's Hotel.

◄ CREMYLL
THE POINT
AND HMS
'IMPREGNABLE'
1904 52417

Cremyll has long
been a crossing
place from the
Rame peninsula to
the Devon side of
the Tamar estuary.
The old HMS
'Impregnable',
moored in this
stretch of water
opposite Devonport
Dockyard, was a
training ship for
boys. A 98-gun
ship of the line, she
was launched at
Chatham in 1810
and took part in the
bombardment of
Algiers six years later.

► CALLINGTON
THE STATION 1908
59723

A steam train arrives from
Plymouth via the Calstock
viaduct soon after the new
standard gauge line was
fully opened in March
1908. Note the engine
shed and the load gauge
in the goods yard. The
station was at Kelly Bray,
just north of the town,
and it survived until 1966.
On the skyline stands
the monumental mine
chimney at the summit of
Kit Hill.

QUETHIOCK
THE CELTIC CROSS 1908 59763

This ancient four-hole cross was restored and placed at the edge of the churchyard in 1881. While Mylor claims the tallest cross in Cornwall, Quethiock's has more stone visible above ground. Today the cross is shaded by trees, but the cottage behind, known as Well House, is still recognisable.

▶ DOWNGATE
THE VILLAGE 1908
59719

All is deserted except for the little girl and pram outside the post office and F Griffin's store. The dominating building is the Bible Christian Chapel, built to serve this rural hamlet and the surrounding district near Kelly Bray and Callington.

▶ CALLINGTON
CHURCH HILL 1908
59727

Entering the town from Kelly Bray and the north, the road climbs towards the early 15th-century St Mary's church. Note the cobbled pavement on the right.

◀ LANDRAKE
NOTTER BRIDGE,
THE RIVER AND THE
SPORTSMAN'S ARMS
C1960 L296317

The Sportsman's Arms
Inn, beside the old
road and bridge over
the River Lynher,
was by-passed by a
new bridge in 1961
during major road
improvements when
the Tamar Bridge was
opened at Saltash.

MENHENIOT
THE VILLAGE 1912
64607

A few miles outside the market town of Liskeard, but away from main roads, this village has largely escaped modern developments. The church of St Lalluwy has a 13th-century tower; the needle spire was added by the 15th century, when the rest of the church was rebuilt.

The distinguished market town of Liskeard reached the height of its prosperity when the copper mines, at the edge of the wild wastes of Bodmin Moor at Caradon Hill, were working at full capacity. Great Western trains thundered through Liskeard bound for Penzance, carrying travellers to within ten miles of Land's End.

LISKEARD
MARKET STREET 1906 56301

Just as it does today, the Italianate clock tower of the Guildhall dominates this view looking towards the steep Pike Street. All is quiet save for a trader making a delivery. No shoppers are attracted to either Morcom's printers, stationers and fancy warehouse on the left, or to Wenmoth's typical hardware and ironmonger's shop opposite.

▶ LISKEARD
THE POST OFFICE
1912 64621

This new post office
has been opened
recently at the corner
of Baytree Hill and
Windsor Place. Note
the high telephone
pole behind the
building, and the
recently built tower
of St Martin's church
in the distance. Postal
services remained
here until 1963,
when a modern post
office was opened on
The Parade.

◀ LISKEARD
LAMELLION 1907 58803

This hamlet down in the
East Looe river valley a
mile from Liskeard was
once a small centre of
industry. The corn mill
is on the extreme left,
while out of shot is a large
wool combing mill which
brought prosperity for a
while. The photograph
is taken from a bridge
over the Liskeard to Looe
railway - Lamellion still
boasts the tiny platform of
Coombe Junction Station.

▲ LISKEARD, CHEESEWRING VILLAGE 1908 59771

This hamlet of miners' cottages at Minions was first known as Cheesewring Railway because the line of that name passed through in 1846. John Gerry's Cheesewring Hotel on the left was the highest hostelry in Cornwall at just under 1,000ft above sea level. It is still open today. The railway and mines have long since closed, but visitors come here to explore the moors and the famous Cheesewring rocks.

ST CLEER
THE VILLAGE 1890
24471

This sizeable village, close by Liskeard, sprawls along a hill-top surrounded by high moorland. All around are the ruins of engine houses and copper mines.

THE TAMAR AND THE EAST

▼ DOBWALLS, THE VILLAGE 1931 84121

Just one motor car heads down through the village for Liskeard along a road that is now the extremely busy A38. Note the telephone poles laden with many wires, a sight no longer seen today.

► DOWNDERRY
ST GERMANS HUT
1890 23753

The balconied St Germans Hut was a shooting box belonging to the Earl of St Germans, set high on the cliffs about a mile east of Downderry. In the 1920s a visiting permit could be obtained from the steward at the family seat of Port Eliot, St Germans, and 'if warning be sent to the Hut, a simple meal can be prepared.'

◄ DOWNDERRY
FROM THE
SEASHORE 1930
83310

This is what children
of all ages like best:
fishing about in the
rock pools at low
tide. The long village
of Downderry stands
precariously on a
shelf between the
inland hills and a
sea-washed cliff edge.

► SEATON
THE BEACH 1935
86935

Holidaymakers and
day trippers have been
drawn to the sandy
beach at the mouth
of the Seaton valley.
Facilities on the far side
include Pearce's Café
and the Eddystone
Hotel, while tents and
caravans of the period
can be seen in the
valley floor on the left.
Downderry village is
alongside the coast road
in the distance.

THE TAMAR AND THE EAST

The ancient fishing town of Looe is divided in two by the Looe estuary. In former times, Looe was an important port for the export of copper ore and granite, and is still a major fishing town.

LOOE, THE QUAY 1888 21311

Fishing luggers are moored alongside the quay at West Looe at high tide, and are preparing to leave for the fishing grounds. Fish baskets are loaded on the nearest vessel.

**LOOE
FROM THE SOUTH 1893
32361**

The narrow sheltered harbour at Looe is seen to good effect from near Hannafore. There are sailing ships and fishing boats alongside the quays at East Looe, with warehouses and a fish cellar in the foreground. This view shows how the town is packed into the level ground between the harbour and steep hillside. The fine bridge across the harbour replaced an older one in 1853, and the tide reaches far beyond.

LOOE, THE LOOE HOTEL 1908 59753

The size of the Looe Hotel in Fore Street reflects the growing tourist industry, which was stimulated at Looe by a railway branch that had been connected to the main line system just seven years before. In 1897 the Looe Hotel was said to be the largest in the district, 'replete with accommodation to meet the requirements of this favourite Watering Place'. The tall stone building on the left is the Guildhall of 1877, and on the right is Richard Pearce's tailor's and outfitter's shop.

THE TAMAR AND THE EAST

LOOE, FISHERMEN 1906 56415

LOOE
THE PIER 1906 56390

The fishermen are standing on 'Little Pier'. We are looking upstream at half tide towards West Looe on the far side of the harbour. On the extreme left is a wall supporting the cliffside road out to Hannafore, 'a developing residential estate facing the open sea.'

THE TAMAR AND THE EAST

▲ POLPERRO
THE HARBOUR 1901 47792

Polperro is arguably the most picturesque fishing village in Cornwall, and it has long been a favourite with artists and day trippers. Smuggling was important in days gone by. Here, the fishing fleet is home, packed behind the breakwater. The crane (centre right) was used to position long timbers across the harbour entrance to provide shelter during rough weather; today a swinging gate performs the same function.

▶ POLPERRO
THE HARBOUR 1924 76331

A few sailing fishing boats remain in the harbour at this date, while two fishermen display part of their catch on the quay.

Polperro's east facing harbour entrance, protected by twin piers, is sheltered from westerlies, but in 1824 a mighty easterly storm demolished the breakwaters and wrecked the fishing fleet.

▲ POLPERRO
CRUMPLEHORN MILL 1908 59751

Here we see the old corn mill deep in the valley at Crumplehorn in working order, with its overshot waterwheel fed by the trough of a launder. Today the mill has been turned into an inn, and the fields below the steep road have been laid out as a car park for visitors to Polperro village that lies down to the right.

◄ POLPERRO
THE JEW'S HOUSE 1924 76345

The fishermen are carrying casks of pilchards from the harbour past one of the many quaint old cottages that make Polperro so attractive to visitors. This building is still recognisable today, although a low wall has replaced the railing and the porch has a window.

CORNWALL

THE TAMAR AND THE EAST

LAUNCESTON FROM THE AIR 1928 AF23648

ANCIENT CORNWALL

THE BEAUTIFUL but harsh landscape of Cornwall is rich in remains of the sacred and ritual sites of ancient peoples, and steeped in myth and legend. The best Neolithic (New Stone Age) monuments are the burial chambered tombs, and some remain intact, while with others only a few raised stones remain to reveal the existence of a single chamber. The Neolithic people are believed to have been the first farmers, no longer following a nomadic lifestyle, but settling in organised social groups and cultivating the land. The famous Carn Brea site, near Redruth, consists of possibly the oldest known Neolithic village in England, and is dated about 3,700 BC. The site subsequently became home to Iron Age inhabitants, who left behind their circular huts and fort ramparts.

On the edge of Bodmin Moor stands the spectacular burial chamber known as Trethevy Quoit (24475). It contained one chamber for the dead and was originally surrounded by a large oval mound; this was last recorded in the 19th century, but has now been obliterated by man and time. Six uprights form the walls, and the massive capstone is 11 feet long.

Near the Madron-Morvah road in west Cornwall, the Neolithic burial chamber of Lanyon Quoit (22985) was restored in 1824 after the capstone fell to the ground during a storm in 1815. It was most certainly originally higher, and might have had a large cairn around it. The chamber would probably have contained the bones of the dead of a local family or tribe, deposited over a long period, which may have been used in rituals.

The period c2,200BC to c500BC is referred to as the Bronze Age. The people understood that the mixture of tin and copper produces bronze, and both metals were in abundance in Cornwall; it may be no coincidence that Cornwall is particularly rich in Bronze Age sites. Nature, the seasons, fertility and death dominated these people. Perhaps the most outstanding monuments they left were the stone circles that are to be found throughout the British Isles. It is generally accepted that most stone circles were 'temples', used for ritual, funerary and astronomical purposes, which were probably linked with the agricultural cycle.

LISKEARD, THE TRETHEVY STONES 1890 24475

LANYON QUOIT 1890 22985

Situated near St Buryan, the Merry Maidens stone circle (22982) is of the Bronze Age; it is one of the most complete stone circles in Cornwall and consists of nineteen stones. The blocks are evenly spaced and are each about four feet high. It is an exact circle, but it appears to have no astronomical significance. The nearby circle of Boscawen-un also has nineteen stones, whilst the small stone circle at Duloe (45909) has only eight stones; it is distinguished because of the size of the stones – one is nine feet high – and the fact they are made of white quartz.

Three Bronze Age stone circles on Bodmin Moor are called the Hurlers, set amongst the old tin mines (45899). They stand in line, and are all over 100 feet in diameter. It is unusual that a few of the stones may have been crudely shaped and are roughly of the same size. They are named 'Hurlers' because it is said that those who profaned the

MEN AN TOL 1890 22986

Men an Tol means 'stone of the hole'; this most famous of Cornish landmarks may belong to the Neolithic period or Bronze Age. Inevitably, legend and myth concerning its use abound; it is said that children were passed through the hole to cure rickets and skin diseases. Adults who were sufficiently slim could ward off fevers by crawling through the hole nine times against the sun! Since this photograph was taken, the site has been tidied and the ground worn smooth by visitors. Some archaeologists claim that the holed stone was the entrance to a Neolithic tomb, or it was part of a Bronze Age circle.

PENZANCE, THE MERRY MAIDENS 1890 22982

This view shows the entrance to the circle on the far side. Legend has it that maidens and pipers were turned into stone for dancing on the Sabbath!

DULOE, THE STONE CIRCLE 1900 45909

LISKEARD, THE HURLERS AND CHEESEWRING HILL 1900 45899

Cheesewring Hill can be seen on the horizon.

Lord's Day by hurling a ball were turned into stone. The granite stone of Bodmin Moor also supports a natural oddity, the impressive outcrop known as the Cheesewring. The summit of Cheesewring Hill encloses a stone fort probably associated with the Neolithic or Bronze Age. The work of nature and man sit comfortably together.

The second highest part of Bodmin Moor is Rough Tor, at 1,311 feet (33593). The Tor has two granite outcrops which nature has weathered to form stacks of impressive bun-like stones; otherwise the moor is bleak and treeless. The summit has a stone fort, where the remains of hut platforms belonging to the Neolithic or early Bronze Age have been found.

Above: LISKEARD, THE CHEESEWRING 1908 59772

Above Left: LISKEARD, THE CHEESEWRING, LONG STONE C1960 L53004

Left: CAMELFORD, ROUGH TOR 1894 33594

HOLY WELLS

Pilgrims seeking their curative powers have long venerated the healing properties of sacred wells. Early Christians would drink or even immerse themselves in 'holy' water. Votive offerings were often thrown into the water; today, tourists often do the same by throwing coins into fountains and wells.

ST CLEER, THE WELL 1938 88595

On the edge of Bodmin Moor, near Liskeard, are several important archaeological sites with Celtic remains. This is St Cleer's Holy Well, in the village named after him. The well is protected by the picturesque 15th-century baptistry erected over it. The trickling waters of this well were said to have special powers to cure madness.

Above: CALLINGTON, DUPATH WELL 1890 24560

The waters of this well were said to be beneficial for whooping cough.

LISKEARD, ST KEYNE'S WELL 1938 88596

This is one of the most famous wells in Cornwall. St Keyne (born AD461) was a Welsh princess who refused to marry. She left her home and, after ridding Keynsham in Somerset of serpents, she eventually arrived in Cornwall. She blessed this well with the power of conferring the power in a marriage to whoever drank of its water first, husband or wife. The custom was immortalised in a poem by the 19th-century poet Robert Southey, who described how one husband rushed to the well straight after his wedding ceremony to find that his wife had already drunk from a bottle of the water that she had brought into the church!

Also in the landscape are several mysterious stones, carved with intriguing inscriptions to long-forgotten heroes. King Doniert's Stone at Liskeard (L53051) is a short granite cross base with a carved interlace design, inscribed on the other side 'Doniert rogavit pro anima', which translates as 'Doniert ordered this for the good of his soul'. He is said have been a king who drowned in AD 875. The taller stone (7 feet) in known as 'The Other Half Stone' and is a cross shaft with carved decoration but a broken-off head. It may be earlier in date and unrelated to the Doniert stone. Both stones stand beside a lane to the north of St Cleer. Near the village of Madron, to the north of Penzance, is the 8ft-tall Men Scryfa, which means 'written stone' (22987). It contains a vertical inscription translated as 'Riolobran son of Cunoval', and dates from the 6th century AD. It is an impressive yet sad monument standing lonely on the bare moor; its meaning is a mystery. The 7-foot-tall inscribed stone at Four Turnings, near Fowey (33593), on the B3269 road, was moved here from Castle Dore but has since been moved nearer the town. It is reputed to be of the 6th century AD. Though the inscription is now too difficult to read, it was said to be 'Here lies Drustanus, the son of Cunomorus.' Some believe that this refers to the legend of Tristan and King Mark.

Liskeard, King Doniert's Stone c1955 L53051

Fowey, The Ancient Inscribed Stone at Four Turnings c1955 F43076

Madron, Men Scryfa 1890 22987

FROM FOWEY TO FALMOUTH

Fowey seamen have been well travelled for centuries - as early as the 16th century they were working Newfoundland's Grand Banks for cod. Not all activities were legal, however - Edward IV had to pay off some European kings and princes after Fowey pirates stole ships and cargoes. The pirates were executed.

FOWEY, FROM HALL WALK 1901 47696

Hall Walk gives an excellent view over the main harbour. Large sailing ships are moored at the buoys opposite the town waiting to go up river to load china clay. Many of the sailing boats and a steam yacht are dressed overall with flags, suggesting that it is regatta time.

FOWEY FROM THE AIR 1939 AFR6284

FROM FOWEY TO FALMOUTH

► FOWEY
MARKET STREET
1888 21249

Here we have a
glimpse of the
church tower
between the houses
of Market Street
in the old heart
of the waterside
town. Note the
gutter in the centre
of the narrow
roadway. Varco the
watchmaker's shop
is on the right,
while J M Williams's
store advertises the
products of the Pure
Soda Water Co.

◄ BODINNICK
FROM FOWEY 1893
32551

The slipway of the ferry
crossing is next to a
wooden boat-building
yard on the Bodinnick
side of Fowey harbour.
The house on the right
is Ferryside, which
just over 30 years later
became the home of the
famous writer Daphne
du Maurier.

FROM FOWEY TO FALMOUTH

▲ FOWEY, PONT QUAY 1893 32562

The quay at the head of Pont Pill, a branch of the Fowey river off Fowey harbour, could be reached at high tide; it was an important trading place with warehouses and limekilns. Seen here discharging a cargo is the ketch 'Rival' - she was the last sailing trader to be built at Fowey, four years before this photograph was taken.

◀ POLRUAN
FORE STREET C1965
P69071

The steep descent to the quay at Polruan has never been kind to traffic, and is better suited to pedestrians. Ice creams and postcards are for sale at the village shop.

FROM FOWEY TO FALMOUTH

▲ POLKERRIS, THE VIEW FROM THE PIER C1960 P65021

Polkerris was once a fishing harbour with a stone pier, but it is now a popular bathing place. The white building close to the beach is the Rashleigh Arms; just to the right is a short slipway up to the old lifeboat house, which was used until 1922 but is now converted to a café and shop.

◀ FOWEY
MENABILLY 1888 21258

This great house near Fowey was the seat of the Rashleigh family. It was surrounded by its own wooded grounds, leading down to the sea at Polridmouth Bay. Daphne du Maurier lived here between 1943 and 1967, and the house was the inspiration for her novels 'Rebecca' and 'The King's General'.

PAR BAY, THE HARBOUR FROM THE MOUNT 1927 *79875*

From the mid 19th century, Par harbour was a major port for the export of china clay. It was first developed in 1840 by Joseph Treffry, who had interests in copper mines, granite quarries, china clay works and a canal and tramway to Luxulyan. In this photograph we see two steam coasters and a sailing vessel alongside the main quay, with a steam tug at the nearest berth. Industries attracted to the harbour site included the tall flour mill, while timber has been imported at the quay on the right.

The opening line of Daphne du Maurier's 'Rebecca' is one of the most famous in English literature. "Last night I dreamt I went to Manderley again."

◀ ST BLAZEY FORE STREET C1965 *S8054*

The Palace cinema and bingo hall dominates this view. One of the films showing is 'The Longest Day', which dates this scene to the early 1960s. The cinema has since been converted to flats.

FROM FOWEY TO FALMOUTH

LOSTWITHIEL
ON THE ROAD TO
RESTORMEL CASTLE
1906 56431

Labourers have been
clearing coppice wood
from a fallen tree beside
the lane from Lostwithiel
to Restormel Castle.
Motorists drive this way
today to visit the shell
keep of the medieval
castle standing high
above the Fowey valley.
The castle came into the
hands of the Duchy of
Cornwall at the time of
the Black Prince.

FROM FOWEY TO FALMOUTH

LOSTWITHIEL
NORTH STREET 1906
56422

The absence of traffic allows the children to loiter safely in the street. Note how the cobbled pavement beside the churchyard wall on the left contrasts with the more modern kerbed paving across the road. At the top of the hill we can see the dome atop the Methodist Free Church in Queen Street.

LERRYN, THE RIVER 2003 L37701

Here we see that the tide has surged up the River Fowey and has filled the broad, tree-lined River Lerryn. The beautiful village is thronged with visitors in summer, and the river full of small boats and canoes. In the winter, however, the creek is a brooding, atmospheric place, with the massed trees hanging heavily over the dark waters of the River Lerryn and many of the cottages empty.

LUXULYAN
THE VALLEY 1907 59364

The beautiful Luxulyan valley has great rounded granite boulders among the trees on its wooded slopes, and at one point it is crossed by a stone viaduct completed by Joseph Treffry in 1842 to carry both a tramway and a water course. This magnificent structure, seen here dominating the valley, was the first viaduct to be built in Cornwall.

BODMIN, MOUNT FOLLY SQUARE 1894 33552

The Shire Hall of 1837 is on the right. The County Assizes were once held here, but today part of the building contains the town's Tourist Information Centre. The building across the square behind the fountain is now Barclays Bank.

▶ BODMIN
FORE STREET 1931
84355

The Market House was built of granite in 1839-40 for the sale of meat, poultry and butter, and the four carved ox heads above the pillars (left) are a notable feature of the street frontage. Bodmin's small fire station was housed in part of the market in 1931. The Town Arms Hotel next door has since closed.

BODMIN
BEACON HILL OBELISK 1894
33559

This prominent granite landmark above the town is 144 feet high. It was built in 1857 in memory of Lieutenant General Sir Walter Raleigh Gilbert, a notable commander of the Bengal Army in the Indian campaigns of 1845-46. He died in 1853, and an inscription at the base of the monument records his service to the nation.

▲ BODMIN, LANHYDROCK HOUSE 1890 24492

Lanhydrock House, once the seat of the Robartes family, is now one of the National Trust's best-loved Cornish properties. The north wing on the right is dated 1636, and contains an impressive long gallery with a decorated plaster ceiling. The rest of the house and the south wing were badly damaged in a fire in 1881, but they were rebuilt in the same style three years later.

◄ ST AUSTELL
BLOWING HOUSE VALLEY
C1884 16759

Looking south just outside the centre of St Austell we see one of I K Brunel's timber viaducts on stone piers built in 1858 for the new Cornwall Railway. The Great Western Railway replaced it with an arched viaduct 40 years later, but the old piers still remain alongside. The title of this photograph refers to the old tin smelting mill just upstream, which used water power to drive the furnace bellows.

*S*t Austell has been branded 'an old fashioned and somewhat gloomy town' by a Victorian guidebook. Its prosperity derives almost entirely from the china clay industry.

ST AUSTELL
FORE STREET 1912 64750

Two prams represent the only traffic in St Austell's attractive shopping street in this scene, which is dominated by the richly carved tower of Holy Trinity church. On the left, the windows of Lee's drapers shop display a sale of costumes, blouses and millinery, with many hats filling the right-hand window.

FROM FOWEY TO FALMOUTH

ST AUSTELL
THE RAILWAY STATION 1912
64752

An up train is about to depart for Plymouth. This view is rich in detail, including the station buildings, the footbridge, a water tower, semaphore signals, lamps and very tall telegraph poles. There is a large goods siding and shed to the left (now the bus station), while on the right are smaller sidings with animal pens, a loading gauge and a shunting signal. A tank engine with a goods train waits for the main line to clear.

PENTEWAN, GENERAL VIEW 1912 64777

The little dock at Pentewan was an important shipping place for china clay after a railway was built down the valley from St Austell in 1829. Coal was imported for St Austell. A village grew up around the dock – we can see the school on the right. The Pentewan Railway closed in 1918, and the harbour soon became blocked and disused.

FROM FOWEY TO FALMOUTH

PENTEWAN, THE SANDS C1955 P37061

This photograph shows camping and caravan holidays 1950s-style, both a holidaymaker's paradise beside the sea and a planner's nightmare. It captures the designs of the tents and caravans of the period, all set down at apparent random, a far cry from what is normally seen on campsites today.

DID YOU KNOW?

Mevagissey was originally known as Porththilly, but was renamed after Saints Meva (or Mewan) and Issey. Its first pier was built in the 15th century, but the town really grew in Napoleon's time when it doubled in size owing to the fishing and smuggling boom.

MEVAGISSEY, LEAVING HARBOUR
1920 69802

A small fishing boat sails out to the fishing grounds in St Austell Bay past the lighthouse on the end of the South Breakwater. The days of sail were numbered, and soon most fishing boats had engines installed.

MEVAGISSEY, THE HARBOUR 1898 41398A

These fishermen have returned to harbour and are sorting the fish caught in their drift nets.

FROM FOWEY TO FALMOUTH

▲ TRURO
WESLEYAN COLLEGE FROM THE BRIDGE 1890
24133

Now known as Truro School, the college was
founded on the hill overlooking the city 10 years
before this photograph was taken, 'affording a
thorough English education at a moderate cost'
for up to 120 boarders. It boasted five classrooms,
a dining hall, dormitories, a sick room and a
chemical laboratory. See how the river comes right
up to the quays in the heart of the city - all of this
was later covered over to become a car park.

◄ TRURO
BOSCAWEN STREET 1923 73618

The bustling centre of Truro is paved with
granite setts, and running water flows in the
gutters. Barclays Bank dominates the west end,
while Lemon Street can be seen emerging on the
extreme left. In the centre of it all a policeman on
point duty waits for traffic to direct. Behind him,
there is a Pickfords horse-drawn removal wagon.

FROM FOWEY TO FALMOUTH

TRURO
CALENICK VILLAGE 1912
64745

The little hamlet of
Calenick lies a short
distance south of Truro,
in a valley bottom on the
old road to Falmouth.
Here beside the old lane
is one of the few thatched
cottages.

FROM FOWEY TO FALMOUTH

▼ TRURO, CALENICK VILLAGE 1912 64744

The clock tower on the far side of the bridge belonged to an important tin smelting works which operated throughout most of the 18th and 19th centuries before closing in 1891. The tin ore was brought from the local mines, and the finished ingots of 'white tin' were shipped from Truro.

▶ FEOCK
THE POST OFFICE 1936
87529

A thatched cottage is the post office. A sign on the rickety telegraph pole advertises a public telephone, and fixed to the nearby wall is a bus timetable proclaiming that this is a fare stage. Feock is on a peninsula at the head of the Carrick Roads on the Fal, and without a car the bus would be the only way to get to Truro.

TRURO MALPAS FERRY AND THE TRESILLIAN RIVER 1912 64738

The ferry boats, one of which could take a horse and cart, were rowed across to Malpas Passage, a narrow peninsula at the confluence of the Tresillian and Truro Rivers, both long branches of the Fal estuary. When the tide was low, pleasure steamers from Falmouth landed their passengers here for Truro.

► ST JUST IN ROSELAND KING HARRY FERRY C1955 S24009

The Fal narrows at King Harry Passage, where a ferry provides a short cut from Truro to St Mawes and the Roseland peninsula. This is Ferry No 4, which was converted from a landing craft in 1951 and worked until the 1960s. It has carried a full load of cars, which are beginning to drive off onto the Roseland shore. We can see cottages at Trelissick on the far side.

FROM FOWEY TO FALMOUTH

FALMOUTH
PENDENNIS HEAD FROM TREFUSIS
1895 37042

Henry VIII's Pendennis Castle stands proud on the headland which gives shelter to the dock area of one of the great natural harbours of the world. A shipyard developed here from 1860, and by the late 19th century there were breakwaters, repair facilities and two dry docks of 350 feet and 537 feet. The docks grew further, with more dry docks, and today Castle Drive is a popular place to view the shipping. The large block on the right is the Falmouth Hotel, a reminder that Falmouth was also a holiday resort.

FALMOUTH, ARWENACK STREET C1960 F4094

The main thoroughfare through the seafaring town has always been busy with pedestrians and traffic. The Shipping Chemist on the corner of Swanpool Street (left) reflects the maritime function of Falmouth. We are looking towards the centre of town; traffic is barred from further progress by the old-fashioned No Entry signs.

PORTSCATHO, ST ANTHONY'S LIGHTHOUSE C1955 P98097

Guarding the entrance to Falmouth harbour, this lighthouse was completed in 1835 to the design of the Trinity House engineer James Walker, who also designed the famous Needles Lighthouse on the Isle of Wight. The light could be seen 22 miles away by vessels approaching the Lizard Point. Until 1954 a 2-ton bell, the heaviest in Cornwall, was hung below the lantern gallery as a fog signal.

◀ PERCUIL FERRY COTTAGE C1955 P362004

This is the site of an ancient ferry crossing; it linked Portscatho and Gerrans on one side of the Percuil River with St Mawes on the other. It became a landing place for pleasure steamers disembarking passengers, some of whom might walk over the narrow peninsula to visit the open coast at Portscatho.

FALMOUTH, FROM THE AIR 1928 AF21723

MAKING A LIVING

IN THIS remote, rocky western land the Cornish have had to toil particularly hard to win an income, for despite the bounty of the seas and Cornwall's ancient mineral wealth, the rocks and seas have given up their riches grudgingly. The fisherman's lot was fraught with danger, and death was always close by as he battled in his small open boat with monumental tides and storms. The Cornish miners, too, endured a harsh subterranean existence, working away at the unresisting rock face with the most basic of tools and machinery. Both trades encouraged a toughness of spirit and strong local and regional pride.

DID YOU KNOW?

'From Padstow Point to Lundy Light, Is a sailor's grave by day or night.'

St Ives, The Harbour 1925 78658

On the sands the business of the day is under way. Men are gutting the catch and a fish 'jouster' negotiates a price for filling his trap. Soon he will be hawking his wares in local villages, announcing his presence with a boisterous asthmatic roar, produced on a set of leathern bellows.

Mevagissey, The Harbour 1890 27557

Mevagissey boats followed the pilchard shoals, and once landed more fish than any other port in the county. Because of the town's pervading odour of fish it was known familiarly as 'Fishygissey'.

DID YOU KNOW?

In 1896 Newlyn fishermen, who never put to sea on Saturdays or Sundays, rioted in protest at 200 Lowestoft boats who worked at weekends. 2,000 men barricaded the harbour, preventing the East Coast men from putting out to sea, and threw fish overboard. The police could not cope, and 300 soldiers of the Royal Berkshire regiment had to be drafted in to restore order.

CAMBORNE, NEW DOLCOATH MINE 1925 78624

Camborne's massive Dolcoath mine reached a depth of over 3,300 feet. To work it economically many thousands of gallons of water had to be pumped out. Richard Trevithick, who invented the first high-pressure steam pumping engine, was born close by at Pool.

Cornish mines in earlier times produced huge quantities of tin and copper, and powerful mine-owners such as Joseph Treffry bought whole harbours in order to ship copper ores to the smelters of South Wales. Harbours such as Newquay might have eight 100-ton schooners in port at any one time, and towns such as Redruth and Camborne grew up around the industry. However the wealth of the industry was not always reflected in the living conditions of the miners. When John Wesley visited Truro in 1789, he was struck by the extreme poverty he found. 'I could not get through the main street to our preaching-house: it was quite blocked up with soldiers to the east and numberless tinners to the west, a huge multitude of whom being nearly starved were come to beg or demand an increase in their wages, without which they could not live'. Granite and slate were also quarried and exported from small, inhospitable harbours along the coast, at places such as Tintagel, Port Gaverne and Port Isaac.

The coming of the railways to the west brought renewed prosperity to the mineral and ore industries, and increased business for Cornwall's ports. They revolutionised transportation, making it possible for many tons of raw material to be hauled quickly and easily from mines and quarries to waiting ships.

Cornwall's great glories, however, now seem all in the past. By the late 1800s the fishing industry was already in decline, and today Cornwall's harbours are almost empty of working ships, and its mines disused. Only the quarrying of china clay has continued to expand since its origins in the late 1700s. Throughout the county there is continual evidence of lost prosperity and fallen industrial might, with disused engine houses and the remains of mine shafts, quarry workings and tramways littering the landscape. The 85ft ornamental chimney stack for Kit Hill United Mine (59724, page 72) was built in 1858 as a summit landmark to be seen from many miles. After closure in the 1860s, the tin mine was re-opened as

PORT ISAAC, GENERAL VIEW 1895 37023

The ship on the beach is typical of the two-masted coastal vessels that plied their trade in the days before motor vehicles came to be used for the moving of commodities. They were loaded and unloaded by horse and cart – a horse can be seen waiting at the port side of the vessel.

FROM FOWEY TO FALMOUTH

Kithill Great Consols in 1881-85. In the photograph, the stack dwarfs a beam engine house to the right, while less substantial buildings are already ruinous; today the stack stands alone. The weather-beaten engine house seen in P273005 stands on the cliffs above the old tin and copper workings of Wheal Edward; the mine closed in 1893 after 20 miners were drowned when old flooded workings were holed. The remains of the more famous Botallack and Levant mines are just along the coast.

Cornwall is perhaps now better known for its industrial archaeology than its living industry, and relies on tourism for much of the county's economic well-being.

Above: PENDEEN, THE ENGINE HOUSE AT WHEAL EDWARD C1960 P273005

Above Right: CALLINGTON, KIT HILL 1908 59724

Above: CARTHEW, CLAY WORKINGS 1927 79869

Cornwall's china clay industry was established by the 1770s. Down the years, pyramids of waste have scarred the landscape above St Austell, creating an eerie, lunar atmosphere. The quarried kaolin is used in filling and coating paper, and in the manufacture of china and fine earthenware.

Left: ST AUSTELL, CHARLESTOWN 1912 64784

A sailing vessel is berthed alongside the quay. Workmen are shovelling china clay down chutes into the hold. The port was invariably busy, also with cargoes of coal and the sweet-smelling barrel-staves which made the casks for transporting the finer qualities of china clay.

THE LIZARD AND THE FAR WEST

"*How remote now and hidden perhaps for ever were the shining waters of Helford, the green hills and the sloping valleys, the white cluster of cottages at the water's edge. It was a gentle rain that fell at Helford, a rain that pattered in the many trees and lost itself in the lush grass, formed into brooks and rivulets that emptied into the broad river, sank into the grateful soil which gave back flowers in payment.*"

'Jamaica Inn', Daphne du Maurier

HELFORD PASSAGE 1930 83197

The Helford River reaches far inland to cut off the Lizard peninsula from the rest of Cornwall. Here on the north shore, a mile from Mawnan Smith, is the ferry place for foot passengers wishing to cross the estuary to Helford village on the Lizard side. A small van is making a delivery.

THE LIZARD AND THE FAR WEST

MAWNAN SMITH
THE VILLAGE 1930
83188

South-west of Falmouth, Mawnan Smith is at a crossroads where one lane continues on to Helford Passage beside the sheltered waters of the Helford River. Children wait outside the shop, perhaps for a school bus, while a thatcher is working on a cottage roof, his ladder supported half way into the road – a dangerous situation with today's busy traffic. Two watchers stand beneath an extremely large telegraph pole (left).

THE LIZARD AND THE FAR WEST

▼ PORT NAVAS, THE POST OFFICE C1960 P363005

On a creek on the north shore of the Helford, Port Navas was once the shipping place for granite from the quarries around Constantine. In the 20th century it became renowned for the Duchy of Cornwall's oyster farm, said to produce some of the finest oysters in the country. The settlement is little more than a hamlet.

► CONSTANTINE OLD TOWN C1950 C408003

The old village of Constantine was home to the miners and quarrymen who worked the granite for which the parish was famous - small wonder that the walls of some of the cottages were solidly built. The signboard on the pavement near the women and children advertises a fish and chip shop.

THE LIZARD AND THE FAR WEST

Smuggling was a major industry in the 18th century, with vast quantities of contraband passing through little ports such as Coverack. In 1736 the Coverack Customs' boat caught a smuggler carrying 150 ankers of spirits. An anker was 8½ gallons, so the haul represented around 5,500 bottles - and this was not considered a large cargo!

◄ GWEEK
GENERAL VIEW
1904 53044

Gweek lies at the very head of the Helford River. The river is tidal, and although there is nothing but mud here at low tide, it was navigable by small coasters well into the 20th century. Here we see imported timber in a yard on the left. Coal was another import to Gweek.

► COVERACK
FROM THE SOUTH
WEST 1938 88567

Development dating from the 19th and early 20th centuries has crept up the hill away from the little fishing harbour on the east side of the Lizard peninsula. These houses have a view out to the English Channel. Across the bay is Lowland Point.

The Lizard and the Far West

CADGWITH
THE COVE 1931
84285

Cadgwith is an important fishing cove, especially for shellfish; boats are hauled up the beach – there is no quay. Here, some fishing boats have their staysails set up to dry, while a small boat on the beach nearest the sea has an early outboard motor.

CADGWITH, THE VILLAGE 1931 84284

Narrow streets, pretty cottages (some of them thatched), fishing boats on the beach, and all in a beautiful setting on the Lizard peninsula, put Cadgwith on the list of places to visit once road transport had improved. A smart touring car is already causing congestion and interest while negotiating a narrow corner in the village.

KYNANCE COVE 1895
36209

A big sea is running into the famous cove, as if to emphasise the rugged grandeur of the west coast of the Lizard. The pinnacles, islands and coloured serpentine rocks combine to make this picturesque scene a must on every tourist's itinerary. The long Asparagus Island on the left can only be reached across the beach at low tide.

Idyllic scenes such as these belie the harshness of life in Cornish fishing villages in past times. Apart from the obvious hazards of storms and wrecks, failure of the fish stocks for even one season could lead to starvation that was only marginally eased by scraping limpets from the shore.

LANDEWEDNACK, CHURCH COVE C1900 L12501

Church Cove was a pilchard fishing place, with boats hauled up the steep beach, and there was also a lifeboat station here for a while until 1899. Pleasure steamers from Falmouth, such as the 'New Resolute' seen here, called to land passengers in rowing boats. At low tide the visitors clambered out onto the Battleship Rock in the centre of the view.

THE LIZARD AND THE FAR WEST

MULLION
FISHERMEN 1924 76638

Small inshore fishing boats are drawn up at the back of the harbour, where two jetties were built in the 1890s to provide shelter and encourage this local industry. The fishermen are sorting nets and a crab or lobster pot, while three children are posed sitting in their midst reading a book.

HELSTON, THE FURRY DANCE H69401

HELSTON, THE FURRY DANCE H69402

HELSTON, MENEAGE STREET 1931 84219

THE LIZARD AND THE FAR WEST

HELSTON FURRY DANCE

Hundreds of years ago, a fiery dragon flew over the little Cornish town of Helston, dropping a large stone in what is now Angel Yard and frightening the population out of their wits. However, no-one was hurt and the people celebrated their narrow escape by dancing in and out of each other's houses. The stone was eventually used in the building of the Angel Hotel. So runs the legend of the origins of Helston's famous Furry Dance, held each year on 8 May. In fact, the ceremony dates back to pre-Christian times, when many Cornish settlements would have greeted the arrival of summer with a fertility ritual which involved dancing and the bringing of flowers and greenery into the town from the woods outside. The early Christians - presumably working on the principle of 'if you can't beat 'em, join 'em' - subsumed this pagan ritual into their religion, and it is surely no accident that Flora Day (the day of the Furry Dance) is celebrated on the Feast of the Apparition of St Michael, the patron saint of the parish.

Helston's Furry Dance has had its ups and downs - in 1875 it was recorded that only 16 couples danced - but it has remained Helston's very own celebration of the summer, unique apart from the 'Obby 'Oss at Padstow. The 8am Hal-an-Tow ceremony, with adults and children carrying branches and singing 'Summer is come O, and Winter is gone O' is an echo of the earliest Pagan rituals. The children's dance at 10am is a relatively new addition, first danced in 1922 and the only dance to be celebrated through the dark days of the Second World War. The principal dance is at midday, when men in top hats and tails and women in formal gowns weave in and out of shops, houses and gardens accompanied by the Helston Town Band and cheered on by the thousands of onlookers who come from all corners to join the festivities and admire the unchanged beauty of this fine Cornish town.

◀ HELSTON
COINAGEHALL STREET 1913
65941

This interesting scene at the top of the principal highway through Helston shows the granite classical-style Guildhall of 1839 behind the covered delivery wagon. The Cornish Bank is beyond, and beside it an omnibus has begun to ascend Wendron Street. One feature of Helston is the fresh water flowing in the gutters, which we can see on the right where a handful of heavily dressed women pose on the wide pavement outside a variety of shops.

THE LIZARD AND THE FAR WEST

◄ PORTHLEVEN
THE OUTER HARBOUR
1911 63641

The fishing fleet is setting sail, and the watchers on the pier are dressed smartly, most notably the lady in the foreground. Porthleven was developed as a port to serve the mining industry, but the expected traffic in mineral ore never materialised. Nevertheless, it gave good shelter to a fishing fleet. The pier, which was rebuilt after a storm in 1824, has a guiding lamp that can be raised up a pole once lit.

HELSTON, THE MONUMENT 1895 36190

This Gothic archway in granite ashlar with four tall octagonal pillars is a landmark that can be hardly missed at the foot of Coinagehall Street. The inscription above the arch proclaims: 'To the Memory of Humphry Millett Grylls'. It was erected to this local worthy in 1834, and paid for by public subscription. The surrounding iron railing has since been removed.

◄ CAMBORNE
MARKET PLACE 1922 73300

Thomas's hardware and ironmonger's shop (left) is at a good corner site, with a large display of wares, while opposite, E R Jones is a 'home and foreign outfitter'. Perhaps the shop supplied the needs of emigrating tin miners, for this was the period when the great Dolcoath Mine closed. Down Commercial Street is the Market House, with a clock tower built by John Francis Basset in 1866. The Bassets of Tehidy were important mineral lords in this once-great copper and tin mining centre.

CAMBORNE, DOLCOATH MINE, NEW SHAFT 1902 49120

The new Williams' Shaft, begun in 1895, is at the time of the photograph still being sunk to develop new sections of the main tin lode, and it was to reach a depth of 550 fathoms (3,300ft) when the mine closed in the 1920s. Having been important for copper, Dolcoath became Cornwall's most productive and deepest tin mine. This shaft, fitted with the latest winding equipment, was named in honour of the chairman of the mine directors.

▶ REDRUTH
WEST END 1902 49113A

We are looking up the hill from the centre of town towards Camborne. Notice the tram (advertising the Cornish Post newspaper) parked at the terminus of the newly opened Camborne and Redruth Tramway - this small operation lasted until 1927. Opposite is Salter & Son's carpenters' workshops, while on the same side of the road are the Western Hotel and the Royal Standard Inn.

◄ REDRUTH
FORE STREET 1922
73283

Today, it would be difficult to stand for long in the middle of this road junction at the bottom of town; here West End meets Fore Street and Penryn Street (right). The town clock tower dominates Fore Street as it climbs away from the camera. The splendid street lamp on the corner has since been removed.

◄ ST DAY
FORE STREET C1955
S457001

This interesting mining village, almost a town, developed in the 19th century close to the great copper mines of Consolidated and United Downs. Terraces of miners' houses form a triangle in Fore, Scorrier and Telegraph Streets. Here in Fore Street the shops include the post office and a hairdresser. A parked motor bike and sidecar is the only traffic.

THE LIZARD AND THE FAR WEST

MARAZION
ST MICHAEL'S
MOUNT c1960
M26011

This photograph was taken from above the town of Marazion; the view shows clearly how the famous Mount is reached by a causeway at low tide. Legend has it that Mediterranean traders came here to Ictis (as the place was called then) to trade for tin.

MARAZION, THE VILLAGE 1920 69756

Climbing out of Marazion on the way towards Helston, it was still possible at this date to drive two horses on the wrong side of the road with little fear of a collision. On the right is a welcome water point and drinking trough.

THE LIZARD AND THE FAR WEST

PENZANCE
THE BOWLING GREEN 1920 69739

There seems to be some dispute as these players pose on the bowling green, while a small audience of no doubt critical ladies watches close to them. Note also the small sign reading 'please keep off the grass'! The sea is near by, and Newlyn can be seen in the distance.

DID YOU KNOW?

The town of Marazion was known in Victorian times for its cultivation of a particularly delicious species of turnip.

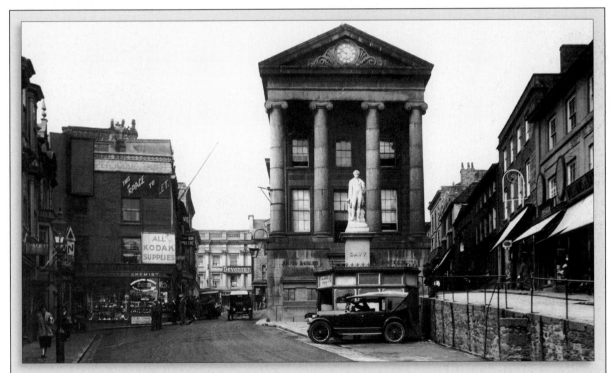

PENZANCE, MARKET JEW STREET 1925 78635

The top end of the main street in Penzance is dominated by the impressive classical frontage of the Market House and Old Town Hall, erected in 1837. Here stands also the white marble statue of Sir Humphry Davy (1778-1829), the town's famous son, whose best-known invention was the miner's safety lamp. The memorial on a granite plinth inscribed 'Davy' was erected in 1872 close to his birthplace.

THE LIZARD AND THE FAR WEST

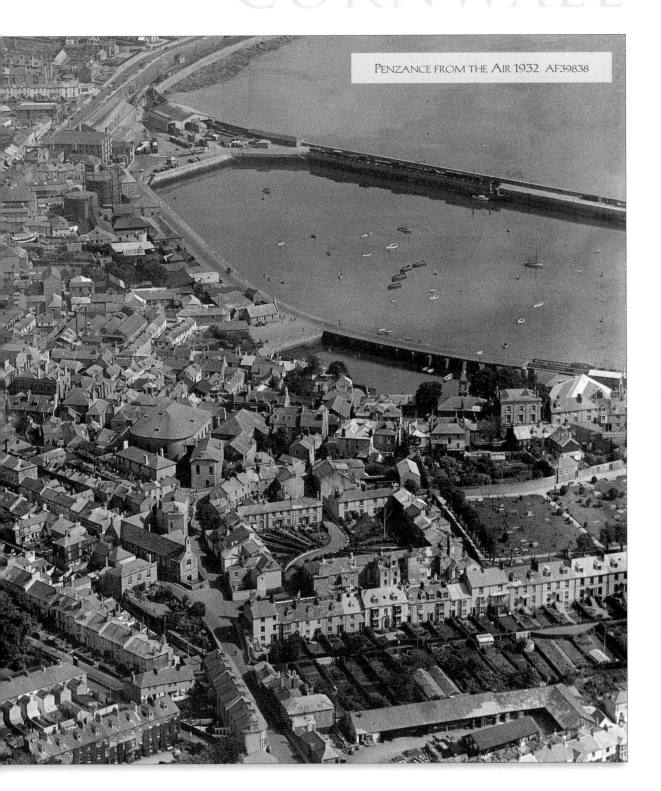

PENZANCE FROM THE AIR 1932   AF39838

THE LIZARD AND THE FAR WEST

Penzance was 'a place of good business, well built and populous, has a good trade, and a great many ships belonging to it', according to Daniel Defoe, when he visited it in the early 18th century.

PENZANCE
THE PROMENADE 1906 56508

A bracing walk along the promenade is part of the holiday at a seaside resort such as Penzance. Long skirts are not best suited to the wind, as we can see from these ladies passing the Queen's Hotel. The seaside flavour is completed by the bucket and spade shared by the two girls.

Newlyn
The Harbour 1908
61241

Boats are drawn up on the beach under the walls of the fishing township, and their nets are drying on the rails beside the slipways. At the top of the first slip is John Reseigh's grocery store, which advertises 'shipping supplied'.

PAUL, THE VILLAGE C1955 P127005

Paul is the mother village for Mousehole, which lies down on the coast below. Regent petrol is served at the village garage on the right, and a single milk churn stands on a wall opposite where it waits to be collected for the creamery.

The poet Dylan Thomas tarried awhile in Mousehole, and married his sweetheart Caitlin at Penzance Registry Office in 1937. He described Mousehole as 'the loveliest village in England'.

MOUSEHOLE, THE HARBOUR
1927 79945

MOUSEHOLE, JEFFERY YARD 1931 84252

Boot and shoe repairs are undertaken in these premises in one of the back yards in the cramped village of Mousehole. Perhaps it is Mr Jeffery himself who is posing at the steps in the foreground.

The last natural speaker of the Cornish language was Dorothy 'Dolly' Pentreath. She died in 1777, and is commemorated with a memorial in Paul's churchyard.

Above Left: MOUSEHOLE, DOLLY PENTREATH OF MOUSEHOLE 1903 49960A

Above Right: PAUL, MEMORIAL TO DOROTHY PENTREATH C1955 P127002

THE LIZARD AND THE FAR WEST

► ST BURYAN
THE CROSS 1908
61267A

This ancient cross head bearing a crude carving of a crucifix must pre-date the church by many centuries. The texture of the coarse granite of the district can be seen in the steps. St Buryan is the largest settlement in this southern part of the Land's End peninsula, and its church tower is a landmark from many miles away.

PORTHCURNO
THE CABLE STATION C1883
16050

The Eastern Telegraph Co's large cable station was established in the valley just inland from the beach at Porthcurno, where undersea cables came ashore. A tennis court was laid out for the exercise of the workers who were stationed at this lonely spot. Note also the allotment gardens behind the station. This remote spot in the far south-west corner of Britain has played a major role in world communications and commerce.

THE LIZARD AND THE FAR WEST

▲ PORTHGWARRA, THE COVE AND THE CAVES 1908 61263

There is just space to bring a few open fishing boats between the rocks to a slipway at this little cove down by the granite cliffs of Gwennap Head. This is a rugged and treeless landscape, where the settlement consists of a few fishermen's houses and a small thatched croft.

◀ LAND'S END 1890 23002

It is fair weather, and a ketch is making good progress under sail as she passes between the rocks of the Longships Lighthouse and Land's End. Note the souvenir seller lurking by the rocks on the right to catch unwary tourists.

THE LIZARD AND THE FAR WEST

LAND'S END, GOG AND MAGOG 1927 79985

Several rock formations around Land's End were given names, which certainly enhanced the place's interest to tourists. These two are named after mythical giants, while other rocks have been given names such as Dr Syntax's Head.

3,147 miles from New York, England's most westerly point of Land's End was named Belerion, or Seat of Storms, by the Romans. Painted by (among others) Turner, written about by (among others) Ruskin, and with the Isles of Scilly visible on the horizon on a clear day, it is a dramatic place despite the hordes of tourists.

THE LIZARD AND THE FAR WEST

LAND'S END
THE MOST
WESTERLY POST BOX
IN ENGLAND C1955
L13085

This is not only the most westerly but perhaps also the most ugly and ill-sited post box in England, but it is clearly a place to post those souvenir postcards after a long cycle ride – perhaps from John o'Groats.

LAND'S END, THE FIRST AND LAST HOUSE C1925 61290B

This must be the most visited and certainly the best placed souvenir and refreshment shop in Cornwall, just a stone's throw from the tip of Land's End. We can see an extension on the right-hand side of the original small house, reflecting the increasing number of tourists who were then coming here.

THE LIZARD AND THE FAR WEST

Artists such as Ben Nicholson, Barbara Hepworth, Peter Lanyon and Patrick Heron all lived and worked in St Ives, attracted by the unique quality of the light.

LAND'S END
THE FIRST AND
LAST TREE IN
ENGLAND 1908
61282

The district has the first and last house and hotel, so why not a tree? The fact that trees are a rarity in this windswept peninsula makes this more significant. There is a low haystack beyond.

CARBIS BAY 1925 78682

This fine beach of golden sand is seen in its early days as a bathing resort. Mobile beach huts are lined up on the sand, while the beach shop offers ices, chocolates, tobacco, Kodak films and daily papers.

Above: ST IVES
THE OLD SLOOP INN 1906 56541

This popular inn on the harbour at St Ives is said to date back to 1312. In the 20th century it became a favourite haunt of the St Ives artists' colony. There is now a small porch by the doorway. The small slate-hung building on the right stands between Pudding Bag Lane and Fish Street, but was swept away in the 1930s to widen access to the latter.

The village of Zennor near Land's End is home to one of Cornwall's more picturesque legends - that of the mermaid of Zennor. She heard a village boy, Matthew Trewhella, singing in the church, and fell in love with him. She lured him away to live with her under the sea, and he was never heard of again. A woodcarving of the mermaid can be found in Zennor's church.

ZENNOR, THE MERMAID, BENCH END IN THE CHURCH Z1402

THE LIZARD AND THE FAR WEST

ST IVES, BAILEY'S LANE 1906 56545

This is just one of the many narrow streets that are so characteristic of St Ives. The fishermen's cottages on the left have been replaced since, but the cobbles and granite gutter on the right can still be identified. The lane leads down to Fore Street.

THE LIZARD AND THE FAR WEST

ST IVES, WASHING DAY 1927 80066

This scene is almost timeless, for the small courts behind the fishermen's cottages are still the only places to hang out the washing to dry.

CORNISH FOOD AND RECIPES

POLPERRO, THE JEW'S HOUSE 1924 76345
These fishermen are carrying casks of pilchards.

PILCHARDS SEVEN A PENNY 1912 64858

CORNWALL is encircled by water, surrounded by the sea on three sides and separated from the rest of England by the River Tamar. Not surprisingly, the sea has always provided both a living and a staple food for the people of Cornwall. Cornish fishermen netted every fish they could, but the pilchard was the most crucial and sought after. (Pilchards are full-grown specimens of sardines.) The pilchard trade was seasonal, and in July the waters of Mounts Bay, extending in a broad sweep from the Lizard in the east to Lands End in the west, were busy with boats competing for a share in the catch. The lives of whole communities revolved around catching and processing the fish – gutting, barrelling, salting and delivering. Later in the year the boats pursued herring, followed by mackerel in the spring.

Salted pilchards are still produced in the traditional way at The Pilchard Works in Newlyn where the owner, Nick Howell, is also marketing fresh pilchards as fresh sardines. With a new, fashionable image, fresh pilchards are now enjoying a renaissance with British cooks.

One of Cornwall's most famous traditional recipes is that for Stargazy Pie, in which pilchards are placed in a pie dish with their heads resting on the rim. Other ingredients such as herbs and bacon are added, and the fish are then covered with pastry, leaving the heads outside the pie, 'gazing at the stars'. The dish is traditionally linked with

MOUSEHOLE, THE FISHING FLEET AND THE ISLAND 1927 79950

the village of Mousehole, where it is eaten on December 23rd – Tom Bawcock's Eve.

Many years ago, during a long period of bad weather, the Mousehole fishing fleet was unable to leave the harbour, and the village was starving. One brave man, Tom Bawcock, was so concerned that he managed to put to sea and catch just enough fish to feed the village. The fish (some stories say there were seven different varieties) were made into a pie with their heads left on, so that nothing would be wasted.

STARGAZY PIE

Several varieties of fish can be used, such as small mackerel, herring, or pilchards, but pilchards (or fresh sardines as they are now known) are particularly authentic.

6-8 fish, gutted, cleaned and boned, but with the heads and tails left on.

2 eggs

3 rashers of bacon, chopped into squares

Grated zest and juice of 1 lemon

1 onion, finely chopped

Seasoning – salt, pepper, parsley and tarragon to taste.

500g (1lb) shortcrust or flaky pastry

MOUSEHOLE, THE HARBOUR 1927 79948

Grate the zest from the lemon, and reserve. Cut 2 slices of lemon for decoration, then squeeze the juice and reserve. Boil the eggs until soft (not very hard-boiled), and cut into small pieces. Roll out half the pastry and line the bottom of an 8" (200mm) pie dish. Arrange the pilchards in the pie dish like the spokes of a wheel, leaving the heads on the rim. Fill the gaps between the fish with the mixture of chopped onion, bacon, eggs and seasoning. Pour over the lemon juice and zest. Cover the pie with the other half of the rolled-out pastry, pressing down well between the heads of the fish to seal, leaving the fish heads outside the lid. Brush pastry lid with beaten egg or milk to give a nice glaze.

Cook the pie in the middle of a pre-heated oven, gas mark 6, 200 C (400 F) for about 30 minutes.

Saffron cakes or buns were once traditionally only made at Easter, as saffron, made from the dried stamens of the autumn crocus, is one of the world's most expensive spices. They are known as a speciality of Cornwall, along with heavy cake, Cornish splits and Cornish pasties. Heavy cake is a slab of fruit cake which is scored on the top to resemble a fishing net; the name may possibly derive from the 'Heva!' call of the man on look-out duty on the cliffs, watching for shoals of fish, although another theory is that it comes from the 'Heave!' call of the fishermen as they hauled in the seine net to the shore. When the women heard this, they knew the men would soon be home for tea, and would make this quick cake.

CORNISH FOOD AND RECIPES

HEAVY CAKE

225g (8oz) plain flour

¼ teaspoon salt

50g (2oz) margarine

75g (3oz) sugar

175g (6oz) currants

75ml (2-3 tablespoons) milk

50g (2oz) butter

Mix the flour and salt in a bowl, and rub in the margarine. Add the sugar and currants, and enough milk to enable the mixture to form a soft dough. Roll out on a floured board into a long strip. Dot half the butter over the first two-thirds of the dough. Fold the bottom third (without the butter) upwards, then fold the top third down over it. Give the dough a half-turn, so that the folds are now at the sides, and roll out again into a thin strip, dot with butter and fold again in the same way as before. Roll out into a square about 1cm (½ inch) thick. Score the top with a sharp knife to make a fishing net pattern. Brush with a little milk, and bake on a greased and floured baking tray above the middle of a hot oven for about 30 minutes, gas mark 6, 200 C, 400 F.

SAFFRON BUNS

¼ teaspoon saffron strands

25g (1oz) yeast

200g (2lb) plain flour

225g (8oz) sugar

¼ teaspoon mixed spice

Pinch of salt

125g (4oz) margarine

125g (4oz) butter

300ml (½ pint) milk

350g (12oz) mixed dried fruit

50g (2oz) chopped mixed peel

Cut the saffron stamens finely, put them into 2fl oz (⅛ pint) warm water, and leave overnight. Mix yeast with two tablespoons of the flour. Mix with 3fl oz (⅛ pint) warm water and one teaspoon of sugar. Leave in a warm place for 30 minutes. Mix flour in a bowl with the sugar, salt and mixed spice. Rub in butter and margarine until the mixture resembles fine breadcrumbs, and add the risen yeast mixture. Warm the milk until it is lukewarm, stir in the saffron mixture and pieces of saffron, and add to the flour mixture. Add the dried fruit and peel. Mix well, and leave in a warm place, covered with a cloth, for several hours, until the dough has doubled in size. Knead and punch the dough down until all the air bubbles have gone. Shape the dough into little buns and let them rise a little, then bake on a greased and floured baking tray for about ½ hour, gas mark 4, 180 C, 350 F.

When cooked, turn on to a wire tray to cool. Serve cut in half with Cornish clotted cream!

A CUP OF TEA AND A SAFFRON BUN 64856

THE NORTH COAST

HAYLE, FORE STREET 1927 80076

Fore Street is in the Copperhouse district of Hayle, which takes its name from a copper works (later a foundry) of the 18th and 19th centuries. The big car is overtaking the little car in a manoeuvre that would be impossible with today's vehicles and traffic volumes. The Cornubia Hotel, in the background with its distinctive porch, remains part of the scene today.

The North Coast

HAYLE TOWANS
TOWANS AND THE
PADDLING POOL
1925 78626

A pool left behind
on the sands by the
falling tide makes
an ideal paddling
place for holidaying
children.

HAYLE TOWANS
TOWANS 1927 80090

With such a fine view across the bay to St Ives, it is little surprise that holidaymakers should have come to camp at
Hayle Towans. This photograph captures the camping scene of the period, with bell tents and early caravans or mobile
homes. A few houses and chalets line the clifftop to ensure the best views.

Portreath was once a thriving little mining port at the terminus of Cornwall's first (horse-drawn) railway.

PORTREATH, THE HARBOUR C1955 P95024

Portreath was built to serve the mines around Camborne and Redruth, and in the 19th century it was busy with sailing ships bringing coal from South Wales and returning with copper ores. Coal was imported down to the mid 20th century – we can see a small Dutch coaster discharging her cargo, with coal heaped on the quayside (centre). There is now a housing estate all over this site in the foreground. The old harbour master's house and dock cottages are on the far side, with more recent housing above. A white daymark stands on the clifftop above the harbour entrance.

PORTREATH
THE PIER 1922 73293

The narrow harbour entrance beneath a treacherous cliff was protected from rough seas by a long pier. It is hard to imagine how sailing ships once came in and out of here.

▲ PORTHTOWAN
GENERAL VIEW 1935 86590

One of the few places on the north
coast with access to a fine sandy
beach and increasingly popular with
surfers, Porthtowan is seen here in
its early years of development and is
hardly recognisable today. These were
pioneering times, with wooden chalets
and bungalows springing up on what
had been a derelict mining landscape.

▶ PORTHTOWAN
THE SWIMMING POOL c1955
P88013

Heavy surf on the beach at Porthtowan
is not the place for smaller children, so
this artificial pool was made among the
rocks as a place for safe bathing. The
water is refreshed at every high tide.

MITHIAN, THE VILLAGE c1950 M227004

This old mining village lies just off the main road between St Agnes and Perranporth. At the junction in the centre of the village stands the Miner's Arms, a fine old building just behind the car (centre left).

PERRANPORTH
THE LOST CHURCH NEAR HOLYWELL
1914 66666

Long buried by the shifting dunes of Penhale Sands, the ruin of an early Christian oratory was discovered in the 19th century. Because of its early date and association with St Piran, it was given protection from the elements and blown sands by the building of this rather unattractive shell. However, it was all deliberately reburied again in 1981.

THE NORTH COAST

PERRANPORTH, THE NATURAL ARCH 1912 64838

Visitors to the great sandy beach at Perranporth can also explore the caves and arches in the cliffs on the west side at low tide. This is not a good place to be caught out by the rising tide, however.

The bay with its golden sands provides sea bathing and surfing for holidaymakers. Note the boys' swimming costumes, and their home-made surf boards. Offshore are the twin Gull Rocks.

CRANTOCK, THE VILLAGE 1912 64819

Two shy little girls have been persuaded to pose beneath a sign advertising Crowle's tea gardens and tea rooms. There is a large parish notice board on the wall behind the lych gate that gives entrance to the churchyard. This is at the end of the village, where a track leads down to a passenger ferry across the Gannel to the Pentire district of Newquay.

CRANTOCK
THE VILLAGE 1928 81288

The village stands on the skyline above the approach to the popular golden sand of Crantock Beach. Untidy parking at the bottom of the lane at the edge of the dunes shows that the problem of cars at beauty spots has been with us since the very start of the motor age. Today, there is an organised car park here.

NEWQUAY FROM THE AIR 1963 AFA115815

► NEWQUAY
CLIFF ROAD 1918 68675

Just horse-drawn traffic, a
bicycle and one distant motor
car are the only vehicles in the
street. This photograph was
taken in the last year of the
Great War, and the pedestrian
on the left is perhaps reading
a newspaper report from the
front. A railway branch from
Par on the main line helped
develop Newquay as a holiday
and bathing resort after it
fully opened in 1876, and the
entrance to the station terminus
is up the street on the left.

The Huer's House was where the
huer waited to spot incoming
pilchard schoals. He would raise
the alarm by crying 'heva! heva!'
and shouting through speaking
trumpets, and would use signals
to direct the fishing fleet to the
shout out in the bay.

The word 'hue' is now obsulete
apart from the phrase 'hue and
cry' but was used in former
times to describe a loud clamour
or public outcry.

NEWQUAY, THE HUER'S HOUSE
1907 59333

▶ NEWQUAY
THE SANDS AND THE ISLAND 1907 59320

The suspension bridge across to a house on the
Island is still a feature of Newquay's Towan Beach.
Note the bathing machines down by the water's edge
on the extreme left.

▼ NEWQUAY, DANCING ON THE BEACH 1912
64790A

Dancing to the accompaniment of the small band
playing on the left is clearly a popular pastime. Note
the lines of canvas bathing tents at the head of the
beach. The whole scene is overlooked by hotels and
boarding houses.

◀ NEWQUAY
LAUNCHING THE LIFEBOAT 1928 81254

Judging by the crowds, this was a
practice launch of the town's self-
righting sailing lifeboat. Newquay had a
lifeboat from 1860, and a new lifeboat
house and launching slip were erected
on Towan Head in 1899. This station
was closed in 1934, although it re-
opened temporarily during the Second
World War.

PORTH
THE VILLAGE 1907 59342

At low tide Porth Beach becomes a sandy inlet on the east side of Newquay, but here the tide is in, with Porth Island and Trevelgue Head seen across the water. Porth means 'harbour', and sailing traders came in here to be beached and unloaded at low tide. The private hotel and boarding house (right) has stables available for visitors.

The decline of the tin and copper mines led to Cornishmen emigrating in search of mining work - known as 'Cousin Jacks', the saying was that you could find a Cornishman at the bottom of any hole in the world.

ST MAWGAN, THE FALCON INN 1907 59345

The village is tucked away in the Vale of Mawgan, five miles north-east of Newquay. The Falcon Inn stands at the bottom of the lane.

It is some 50 years after photograph 59345 was taken, and we are looking up the lane with the village shop and the Falcon Inn on the left. The main differences are the telegraph and electricity supply poles and cables, the Western National bus timetable and the inn's sign, now a coat of arms.

ST COLUMB MAJOR, GLEBE HOUSE AND THE CHURCH 1888 21194

This curious old slate-hung house next to the church dates from 1638. The poster on the wall by the tree advertises shipping to Canada and the United States, popular destinations for Cornish people forced to emigrate when the mining industry declined in the later 19th century. Boots and shoes are displayed in the shop window on the left.

St Columb's most famous son was James Polkinghorne, who divided his time between being landlord of the Red Lion and participating in Cornish wrestling. This was once a major sport: Polkinghorne, as Cornish Champion, fought in front of a crowd of 17,000 when he faced Devon Champion Abraham Cann in 1826.

St Columb Major
Fore Street 1906
56244

Trebilcock's shop is displaying the well-known brand of K shoes and boots. The corner of the imposing Town Hall is on the left, partly hiding the venerable slate-hung King's Arms at the point where Fore Street narrows further. A sign beyond the shop advertises an agency representing the Union Castle Steamship Co for South Africa, to which many Cornishmen emigrated.

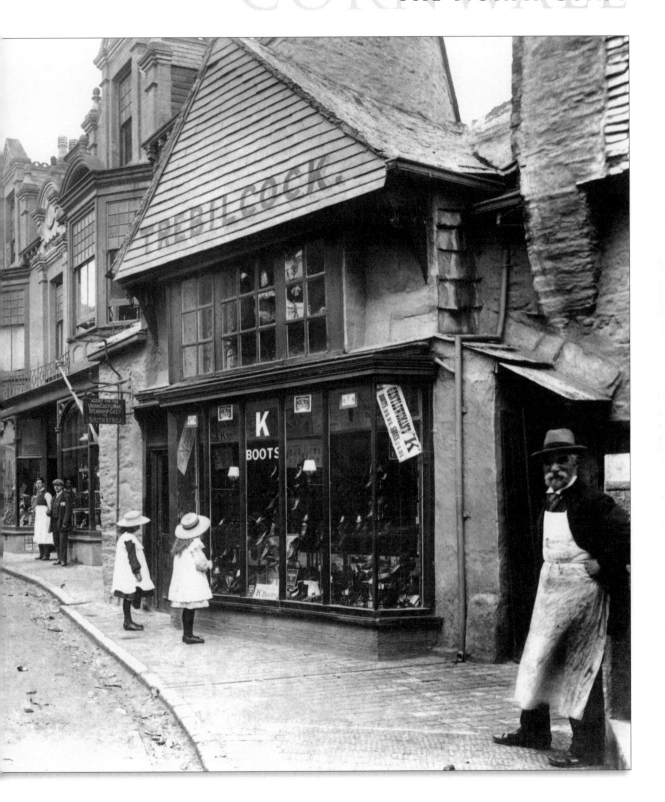

Padstow is still best known for its ancient May Day hobby horse celebrations. The 'Oss is a man dressed in a heavy costume with plumed cap and hooped skirt, and a head-dress with snapping jaws. He is accompanied by a Teaser, singers, dancers and musicians who revive him at intervals. The 'Oss is thought to be a fertility symbol and a woman 'caught' under her skirts is supposed to become lucky or pregnant. The ancient custom starts at midnight on 30 April and continues until 2 May. Since the First World War there have been two horses. They emerge from their 'stables' on May Day morning and are supported by locals wearing white, a buttonhole of spring flowers and a red or blue ribbon according to the 'Oss. Traditional songs are sung until the evening, and maypole dancing follows the day after. The ceremony contibutes to the general liveliness of Padstow today.

PADSTOW, MARKET PLACE 1906 56268

MAY DAY 'DAY SONG'

Unite and unite let us all unite,
For summer is acome unto day,
And whither we are going we will all unite,
In the merry morning of May.

Right: PADSTOW,
THE QUAY 1910 69710

Below: PADSTOW,
THE HARBOUR 1901 47714

By the 18th century Padstow's harbour was so much
obstructed by sand that navigation was difficult.
According to legend, the harbour was cursed by a
mermaid who was shot with a longbow by a Padstow
man. She cast some sand into the sea and foretold that it
would block the harbour.

A MERMAID Z1401

BEDRUTHAN STEPS
1887 20288

This stretch of coast is one of Cornwall's famous beauty spots, with dramatic cliffs and islands all accessible by road from Newquay and Padstow alike. A difficult descent can be made to the golden sand (see the footprints, centre), but this is a very easy place to get cut off by the tide.

The huge foreshore stacks of Bedruthan steps, one of Cornwall's most famous sites, were formed by the erosion of softer rocks around them. However, legend says that these rocks were stepping-stones used by the giant Bedruthan.

BEDRUTHAN STEPS
QUEEN BESS ROCK 1887 20291

Many of the sea stacks and islands at Bedruthan have names, and Queen Bess is the best known of them. It may be said that the upper part also shows a remarkable likeness to the profile of Queen Victoria.

PADSTOW, THE QUAY 1938 88788

By the time of this photograph tourism is taking over from the traditional port activities of fishing and trading, and there are one or two pleasure motor boats moored in the harbour. May's Café (left) is there to serve the needs of visitors to the quayside.

PADSTOW
TREVOSE LIGHTHOUSE 1920 69713

The north coast of Cornwall is extremely hazardous for shipping; after numerous wrecks and petitions to Trinity House, a new lighthouse was built on the Head in 1847 with a range of over 20 miles. The enormous fog-horn trumpet was here from 1913 to 1964, and measured 36 feet long and 18 feet high. A more powerful foghorn replaced it, but its noise caused some people in Padstow to complain.

WADEBRIDGE, THE BRIDGE 1906 56255

The 'longest and fairest' bridge in Cornwall crosses the upper part of the Camel estuary, seen here at high tide. This famous bridge was built by Thomas Lovibond in the late 15th century - it has been widened twice since. After many years of increasing traffic congestion, we may be thankful that it has now been by-passed by a high bridge downstream. This view is looking east from Wadebridge to the Egloshayle side of the bridge.

▶ ROCK
THE VILLAGE 1933
85986

Opposite Padstow on the north shore of the Camel estuary, Rock became increasingly popular with dinghy sailors and holidaymakers between the wars. There are several young holidaymakers and a touring car outside the Rock Hotel.

◄ WADEBRIDGE, CAMELFORD ROAD 1920 69702

A horse looks with interest at the two little boys in the road. The old road to Camelford and beyond, later becoming the A39, climbs steeply up Gonvena Hill from the bridge.

At Wadebridge the Camel is so fast flowing that it is said that there were once chapels on each bank by the ford where travellers prayed for a safe crossing.

▼ POLZEATH, GENERAL VIEW 1925 78836

The surfing resort of Polzeath developed between the two world wars. We can see tents in the distant field, and although there has been more housing since, the beach and its surf remain as magnificent as ever.

The estuary of the Camel is one of Cornwall's greatest natural features, fringed with golden sands and surrounded by rolling farmland. The Camel rises north of Camelford on the edge of Bodmin Moor, and is one of Cornwall's best salmon rivers - a 34lb specimen was caught in the 1920s.

PORT ISAAC
GENERAL VIEW 1895
37025

The Victorian school stands right on the edge of the cliff above the fishing harbour. This view shows the upper part of the village before it was altered by 20th-century developments. Behind we can see the wind-shorn north Cornish scenery with its treeless field hedges.

Apart from fishing, another important source of income for the people of Port Isaac was smuggling. In this they were aided by Port Isaac's maze of narrow streets, or 'drangs', in which they could run the excise men ragged, communicating by a series of coded knocks on the walls of adjoining houses.

ST TUDY, CHURCH TOWN 2003 S835701

This picturesque village sits in a beautiful valley between the Rivers Camel and Allen. Its winding streets and lanes are lined with slate-roofed stone cottages, some colour-washed, their gardens stuffed tight with exotic plants and palms. Here we are looking along the street that encircles the church. In the foreground is the village pump, and on the extreme left the wall of the old forge. Water from the pump was used by the blacksmith to cool down and shrink the red-hot iron tyres he fitted to wooden wagon wheels.

The narrow Trebarwith valley emerges at the north Cornish coast; here Trebarwith Strand presents a good beach of golden sand, but all vanishes at high tide. This is the only beach that is easily accessible for a long way, so it can become busy in summertime. Gull Rock stands offshore.

TINTAGEL, THE CASTLE 1895 36987

The dramatic cliffs and ruined castle at Tintagel have been photographed from many angles over the years. Here we are looking from the 'island' back to the outer ward of the castle, with the access lane down the valley on the left. The building is now a café. The cliffside footpaths have since all changed as a result of rock falls over the intervening century. Another point of interest is the absence of the massive King Arthur's Castle Hotel, which was built soon afterwards on the headland to the left.

THE NORTH COAST

While Boscastle's harbour area is well known to tourists, the true village of Boscastle climbs a steep hill to the south. The village was devastated by a flash flood in 2004, and was the subject of a popular BBC TV series 'A Seaside Parish'.

BOSCASTLE, THE HARBOUR
1893 33606

There is much texture in this detailed composition of one corner of the harbour, made by the slate stones of the breakwater wall, the heavy coiled ropes and the basketwork of the crab pots.

THE NORTH COAST

▼ BOSCASTLE, THE PIXIE SHOP C1960 B149086

Tourist souvenirs are for sale down by the harbour. Note the shelter made from an old boat in the front garden.

DELABOLE
THE SLATE QUARRY 1938 88768

This famous slate quarry is the deepest in England, the result of centuries of work. Although the great days of the 19th century had passed, there were still over 300 men employed here in 1938. Hanging across the quarry is a 'blondin' crane for raising stone from the depths, while in the background a steep incline ascends to the workshops where the slate was split and dressed for market. The houses of the village seem to perch on the very quarry edge.

◄ CAMELFORD
OUTGROUND MILL 1894 33586

Just outside Camelford, which we can see in the background, Outground Mill took the water for its overshot wheel from a side stream. The corn miller at the time was John Harris. The small mill, the miller's house and the allotment behind make a nice group.

Specimens of 'Little Trees', a species of deep water coral so named because of its shape, are sometimes washed up on the sea at Crackington. Local lore says they are a good luck charm, and that having a piece in your house will prevent it burning down.

▶ CRACKINGTON HAVEN
GENERAL VIEW 1931 84321

Being one of the few beaches south of Bude that can be accessed by car ensured that Crackington Haven had its compliment of holiday facilities, such as the hotel we see here with players just visible on its tennis court (left). In past times the beach served as a port, with sailing ships coming onto the exposed beach to be discharged at low tide. The coastal footpath climbs diagonally up to Penkenna Point.

BUDE
THE CANAL AND THE
HARBOUR 1890 23782

The lower end of the Bude Canal has a basin with a sea lock to allow ships to enter and remain afloat. Three vessels are in port, while a fourth one lies aground beyond the lock gates. The Bude Canal was opened in 1826 with the aim of carrying lime-rich sea sand in tub boats to improve the acid farm soils of the hinterland. Sand was dug from the beach and carried up the tramway we can see on the right.

◀ POUGHILL
THE VILLAGE 1938
88753

The post office stores stands on a corner in the centre of the village near the church, and is still trading today. Note the enamel signs advertising Cadbury's 'delicious wholesome' chocolate and Wills's Gold Flake tobacco.

▲ STRATTON, THE BRIDGE 1893 31930

The old bridge crosses the River Neet as it flows towards the sea at nearby Bude. Stratton was formerly more important than Bude, and was a centre for the salt trade.

There is an old rhyme which goes 'By Tre, Pol and Pen, Ye shall know Cornishmen', and these are the most common prefixes in Cornish names. 'Tre' means a homestead or town, 'Pol' means a pool, and 'Pen' means a headland or hill.

◀ KILKHAMPTON
THE VILLAGE 1910
62405

The London Inn (left) is well placed to catch passing trade on the main highway through the village. A single pony and trap contrasts with today's busy motor traffic that passes along this road - it is now the A39. Behind the trees, St James's church is well known for its carved bench ends and a Norman doorway.

THE NORTH COAST

KILKHAMPTON
COOMBE VALLEY MILL
1929 82897

The thatched mill house is deep in the valley about half a mile inland from the beach at Duckpool, and there is just a glimpse of the coast in this view. The earliest parts of the house date from before 1700. This and other cottages at this secluded spot are now leased out for holidays by the Landmark Trust.

MORWENSTOW, THE CHURCH 2003 M100701

This remote church sits hidden amongst trees at the head of a valley leading to the sea. The eccentric Reverend Hawker was vicar here from 1834 to 1875. He was passionately concerned for the fate of shipwrecked sailors, and gave them proper burials - in the centre is the white figure-head of the brig 'Caledonia' that broke up in 1842. Hawker had a deep passion for this church: 'Look without the church - there is the restless old ocean thundering with all his waves ... Look within - all is calm.'

INDEX

FRANCIS FRITH'S
COUNTY
MEMORIES

The Francis Frith Collection Titles

www.francisfrith.com

The Francis Frith Collection publishes over 100 new titles each year. A selection of those currently available is listed below. For latest catalogue please contact The Francis Frith Collection. **Town Books** 96 pages, approximately 75 photos. **County and Themed Books** 128 pages, approximately 135 photos (unless specified). Pocket Albums are miniature editions of Frith local history books 128 pages, approximately 95 photos.

Accrington Old and New
Alderley Edge and Wilmslow
Amersham, Chesham and Rickmansworth
Andover
Around Abergavenny
Around Alton
Aylesbury
Barnstaple
Bedford
Bedfordshire
Berkshire Living Memories
Berkshire Pocket Album
Blackpool Pocket Album
Bognor Regis
Bournemouth
Bradford
Bridgend
Bridport
Brighton and Hove
Bristol
Buckinghamshire
Calne Living Memories
Camberley Pocket Album
Canterbury Cathedral
Cardiff Old and New
Chatham and the Medway Towns
Chelmsford
Chepstow Then and Now
Cheshire
Cheshire Living Memories
Chester
Chesterfield
Chigwell
Christchurch
Churches of East Cornwall
Clevedon
Clitheroe
Corby Living Memories
Cornish Coast
Cornwall Living Memories
Cotswold Living Memories
Cotswold Pocket Album
Coulsdon, Chipstead and Woodmanstern
County Durham
Cromer, Sheringham and Holt
Dartmoor Pocket Album
Derby
Derbyshire
Derbyshire Living Memories
Devon
Devon Churches
Dorchester

Dorset Coast Pocket Album
Dorset Living Memories
Dorset Villages
Down the Dart
Down the Severn
Down the Thames
Dunmow, Thaxted and Finchingfield
Durham
East Anglia Pocket Album
East Devon
East Grinstead
Edinburgh
Ely and The Fens
Essex Pocket Album
Essex Second Selection
Essex: The London Boroughs
Exeter
Exmoor
Falmouth
Farnborough, Fleet and Aldershot
Folkestone
Frome
Furness and Cartmel Peninsulas
Glamorgan
Glasgow
Glastonbury
Gloucester
Gloucestershire
Greater Manchester
Guildford
Hailsham
Hampshire
Harrogate
Hastings and Bexhill
Haywards Heath Living Memories
Heads of the Valleys
Heart of Lancashire Pocket Album
Helston
Herefordshire
Horsham
Humberside Pocket Album
Huntingdon, St Neots and St Ives
Hythe, Romney Marsh and Ashford
Ilfracombe
Ipswich Pocket Album
Isle of Wight
Isle of Wight Living Memories
King's Lynn
Kingston upon Thames
Lake District Pocket Album
Lancashire Living Memories
Lancashire Villages

Available from your local bookshop or from the publisher

The Francis Frith Collection Titles (continued)

Lancaster, Morecambe and Heysham Pocket Album
Leeds Pocket Album
Leicester
Leicestershire
Lincolnshire Living Memoires
Lincolnshire Pocket Album
Liverpool and Merseyside
London Pocket Album
Ludlow
Maidenhead
Maidstone
Malmesbury
Manchester Pocket Album
Marlborough
Matlock
Merseyside Living Memories
Nantwich and Crewe
New Forest
Newbury Living Memories
Newquay to St Ives
North Devon Living Memories
North London
North Wales
North Yorkshire
Northamptonshire
Northumberland
Northwich
Nottingham
Nottinghamshire Pocket Album
Oakham
Odiham Then and Now
Oxford Pocket Album
Oxfordshire
Padstow
Pembrokeshire
Penzance
Petersfield Then and Now
Plymouth
Poole and Sandbanks
Preston Pocket Album
Ramsgate Old and New
Reading Pocket Album
Redditch Living Memories
Redhill to Reigate
Richmond
Ringwood
Rochdale
Romford Pocket Album
Salisbury Pocket Album
Scotland
Scottish Castles
Sevenoaks and Tonbridge
Sheffield and South Yorkshire Pocket Album
Shropshire
Somerset
South Devon Coast
South Devon Living Memories
South East London
Southampton Pocket Album
Southend Pocket Album
Southport

Southwold to Aldeburgh
Stourbridge Living Memories
Stratford upon Avon
Stroud
Suffolk
Suffolk Pocket Album
Surrey Living Memories
Sussex
Sutton
Swanage and Purbeck
Swansea Pocket Album
Swindon Living Memories
Taunton
Teignmouth
Tenby and Saundersfoot
Tiverton
Torbay
Truro
Uppingham
Villages of Kent
Villages of Surrey
Villages of Sussex Pocket Album
Wakefield and the Five Towns Living Memories
Warrington
Warwick
Warwickshire Pocket Album
Wellingborough Living Memories
Wells
Welsh Castles
West Midlands Pocket Album
West Wiltshire Towns
West Yorkshire
Weston-super-Mare
Weymouth
Widnes and Runcorn
Wiltshire Churches
Wiltshire Living Memories
Wiltshire Pocket Album
Wimborne
Winchester Pocket Album
Windermere
Windsor
Wirral
Wokingham and Bracknell
Woodbridge
Worcester
Worcestershire
Worcestershire Living Memories
Wyre Forest
York Pocket Album
Yorkshire
Yorkshire Coastal Memories
Yorkshire Dales
Yorkshire Revisited

See Frith books on the internet at www.francisfrith.com

FRITH PRODUCTS & SERVICES

Francis Frith would doubtless be pleased to know that the pioneering publishing venture he started in 1860 still continues today. Over a hundred and forty years later, The Francis Frith Collection continues in the same innovative tradition and is now one of the foremost publishers of vintage photographs in the world. Some of the current activities include:

INTERIOR DECORATION

Today Frith's photographs can be seen framed and as giant wall murals in thousands of pubs, restaurants, hotels, banks, retail stores and other public buildings throughout the country. In every case they enhance the unique local atmosphere of the places they depict and provide reminders of gentler days in an increasingly busy and frenetic world.

PRODUCT PROMOTIONS

Frith products are used by many major companies to promote the sales of their own products or to reinforce their own history and heritage. Frith promotions have been used by Hovis bread, Courage beers, Scots Porage Oats, Colman's mustard, Cadbury's foods, Mellow Birds coffee, Dunhill pipe tobacco, Guinness, and Bulmer's Cider.

GENEALOGY AND FAMILY HISTORY

As the interest in family history and roots grows world-wide, more and more people are turning to Frith's photographs of Great Britain for images of the towns, villages and streets where their ancestors lived; and, of course, photographs of the churches and chapels where their ancestors were christened, married and buried are an essential part of every genealogy tree and family album.

FRITH PRODUCTS

All Frith photographs are available Framed or just as Mounted Prints and Posters (size 23 x 16 inches). These may be ordered from the address below. From time to time other products - Address Books, Calendars, Table Mats, etc - are available.

THE INTERNET

Already ninety thousand Frith photographs can be viewed and purchased on the internet through the Frith websites and a myriad of partner sites.

For more detailed information on Frith companies and products, look at this site:

www.francisfrith.com

See the complete list of Frith Books at: www.francisfrith.com
This web site is regularly updated with the latest list of publications from The Francis Frith Collection. If you wish to buy books relating to another part of the country that your local bookshop does not stock, you may purchase on-line.

For further information, trade, or author enquiries please contact us at the address below:
The Francis Frith Collection, Frith's Barn, Teffont, Salisbury, Wiltshire, England SP3 5QP.
Tel: +44 (0)1722 716 376 Fax: +44 (0)1722 716 881 Email: sales@francisfrith.co.uk

---

See Frith products on the internet at www.francisfrith.com

FREE PRINT OF YOUR CHOICE

Mounted Print
Overall size 14 x 11 inches (355 x 280mm)

Choose any Frith photograph in this book.
Simply complete the Voucher opposite and return it with your remittance for £3.50 (to cover postage and handling) and we will print the photograph of your choice in SEPIA (size 11 x 8 inches) and supply it in a cream mount with a burgundy rule line (overall size 14 x 11inches).
Please note: photographs with a reference number starting with a "Z" are not Frith photographs and cannot be supplied under this offer.
Offer valid for delivery to one UK address only.

PLUS: **Order additional Mounted Prints at HALF PRICE - £7.49 each** (normally £14.99)
If you would like to order more Frith prints from this book, possibly as gifts for friends and family, you can buy them at half price (with no additional postage and handling costs).

PLUS: **Have your Mounted Prints framed**
For an extra £14.95 per print you can have your mounted print(s) framed in an elegant polished wood and gilt moulding, overall size 16 x 13inches (no additional postage and handling required).

IMPORTANT!

These special prices are only available if you use this form to order. You must use the ORIGINAL VOUCHER on this page (no copies permitted). We can only despatch to one UK address. This offer cannot be combined with any other offer.

Send completed Voucher form to:
The Francis Frith Collection, Frith's Barn, Teffont, Salisbury, Wiltshire SP3 5QP

CHOOSE A PHOTOGRAPH FROM THIS BOOK

Voucher for *FREE* and Reduced Price Frith Prints

Please do not photocopy this voucher. Only the original is valid, so please fill it in, cut it out and return it to us with your order.

Picture ref no	Page no	Qty	Mounted @ £7.49	Framed + £14.95	Total Cost £
		1	Free of charge*	£	£
			£7.49	£	£
			£7.49	£	£
			£7.49	£	£
			£7.49	£	£
			£7.49	£	£

Please allow 28 days for delivery. Offer available to one UK address only

* Post & handling	£3.50
Total Order Cost	£

Title of this book . . . .

I enclose a cheque/postal order for £ . . . . made payable to 'The Francis Frith Collection'

OR please debit my Mastercard / Visa / Maestro card, details below

Card Number

Issue No (Maestro only)   Valid from (Maestro)

Expires   Signature

Name Mr/Mrs/Ms . . . .
Address . . . .
. . . .
. . . .
. . . . Postcode . . . .
Daytime Tel No . . . .
Email . . . .

ISBN 1-84589-113-9   Valid to 31/12/09

Can you help us with information about any of the Frith photographs in this book?

We are gradually compiling an historical record for each of the photographs in the Frith archive. It is always fascinating to find out the names of the people shown in the pictures, as well as insights into the shops, buildings and other features depicted.

If you recognize anyone in the photographs in this book, or if you have information not already included in the author's caption, do let us know. We would love to hear from you, and will try to publish it in future books or articles.

Our production team

Frith books are produced by a small dedicated team at offices in the converted Grade II listed 18th-century barn at Teffont near Salisbury, illustrated above. Most have worked with The Francis Frith Collection for many years. All have in common one quality: they have a passion for The Francis Frith Collection. The team is constantly expanding, but currently includes:

Andrew Alsop, Paul Baron, Jason Buck, John Buck, Jenny Coles, Heather Crisp, David Davies, Natalie Davis, Louis du Mont, Isobel Hall, Chris Hardwick, Neil Harvey, Julian Hight, Peter Horne, James Kinnear, Karen Kinnear, Tina Leary, Stuart Login, Sue Molloy, Sarah Roberts, Kate Rotondetto, Eliza Sackett, Terence Sackett, Sandra Sampson, Adrian Sanders, Sandra Sanger, Julia Skinner, Lewis Taylor, Will Tunnicliffe, David Turner and Ricky Williams.

Elegant home accessories for elegant living

Red rose and yellow rose pillows

Instructions on page 42

Two hibiscus pillows
Instructions on page 47

Scalloped and lace-trimmed doilies

Instructions on pages 48 and 50

3

Three roses with buds pillow

4   Instructions on page 50

Spring bouquet and rose bouquet pictures
Instructions on pages 53 and 56

5

Artichoke table center and place mats

Instructions on page 58

Round tablecloth
Instructions on page 62

Spring garden tablecloth

Instructions on page 64

Anemone wagon mat

Instructions on page 60

9

Piano cover

Instructions on page 69

11

Pillow

Instructions on page 68

Two wall hangings
Instructions on pages 72 and 74

13

Turkish bellflower pillow
Instructions on page 76

Floral bedspread
Instructions on page 77

14

Swan pillow
Instructions on page 80

16

Two fairy tale
pictures and
matching pillow
Instructions on pages 81 and 84

Oval framed picture
Instructions on page 89   **17**

Delicate
and dainty works
of shadow stitch

Pillow
Instructions on page 88

Lampshade
and matching table center
Instructions on page 94

20

Tablecloth
Instructions on page 91

Two dish covers   Instructions on pages 98 and 100

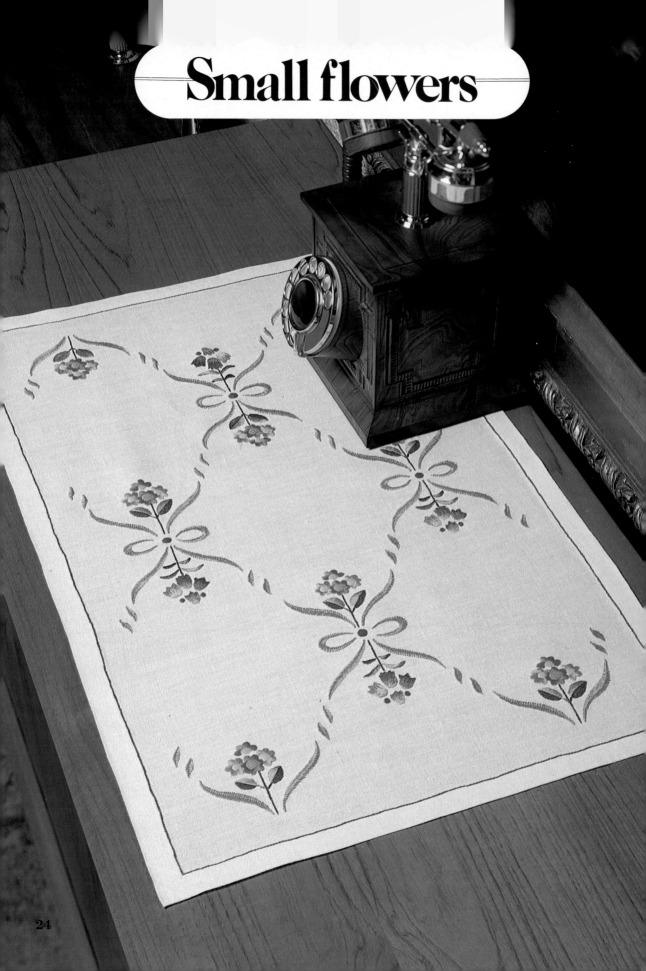

Small flowers

24

Doily
Instructions on page 101

Tablecloth
Instructions on page 101

Tray mat and matching coasters
Instructions on page 104

Blue rose doily and matching coasters

Instructions on page 103

White flowered
table center
and doilies
Instructions on page 106

Place mats and
matching coasters
Instructions on page 108

28

Album cover with angel in the flower garden

Instructions on page 110

Two album covers with three girls and with arabesque design

Instructions on pages 112 and 115

Sachet, evening bag and tissue case

Instructions on pages 114 and 118

Flower basket jewelry box
Instructions on page 119

Two mirror covers and matching tissue box covers

Instructions on pages 122 and 124

34

**Bottle mat and
matching coasters**
Instructions on page 126

35

Sewing box, glasses case and cosmetic case
Instructions on pages 121 and 128

Two pairs of slippers
Instructions on pages 129 and 130

Four birds' pictures
Instructions on pages 131, 132, 133 and 134

Brick house wall hanging

Instructions on page 41

MATERIALS

Fabric: Beige linen for embroidery and lining, 28 cm by 35 cm. Heavy, coarse linen in beige for both sides 22 cm by 35 cm.

Threads: D.M.C. # 25 six-strand embroidery floss. ½ skein each of 420, 422, 869 (hazel-nut brown), 610, 611, 612, 613 (drab), 640, 642, 644, 822 (smoke grey), 839, 840, 841, 842 (beige brown), 3022, 3023, 3024, 3045, (beige), 433, 434 (umber), 451, 452, 453 (seagull grey), 645, 646, 647, 648 (beaver grey), 3032, 3033 (dark brown), 830 (copper green), 3051, 5053 (green), 926, 927, 928 (myrtle grey), 3012, 3013 (sage green) and 580 (golden green).

One rod, 1 cm in diameter and 26 cm long. White linen thread, 20g.

FINISHED SIZE: See diagram.

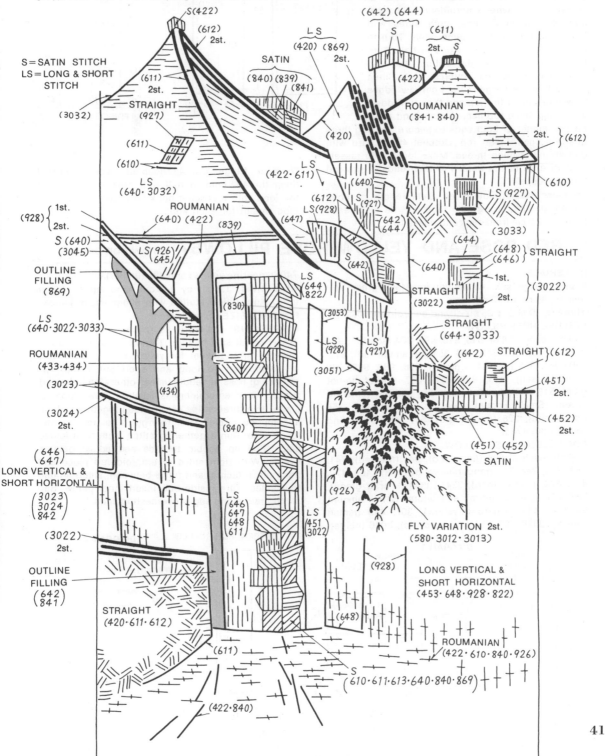

41

DIRECTIONS: Cut fabric as indicated (see diagram). Trace actual size pattern. Transfer design to fabric. Work all embroidery in outline stitch with one strand of floss in needle unless otherwise indicated. Note that walls, roofs and fences are to be shaded in beige-brown, just like in painting a picture, and that each brick is to be embroidered with the shades of lightness and darkness alternately. Work middle part of left fence and whole right fence in long vertical and short horizontal stitches at random. Press, when embroidery is finished. Join embroidered piece, both sides and lining together. Press seams open. Turn to right side and fold both sides in half. Turn raw edges inside at the bottom and slip stitch closed. Attach doubled white linen thread to make fringe. Turn 1 cm raw edges to wrong side at the top and then turn down 3 cm. Slip stitch top hem in place and overcast a quarter of both ends to secure, leaving three quarters open. Insert rod. Crochet 40 cm cord with one strand of linen thread. Make loops with tassels at both ends of the cord. Put both ends of the rod through loops.

To make tassel: Cut fifteen 8 cm length of linen thread, double through the loop and tie all threads together 2.5 cm from each end. Make two.

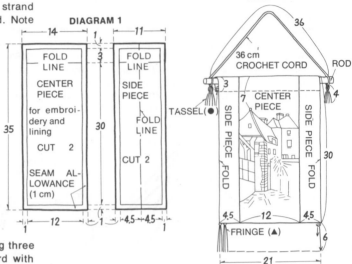

To make fringe: Cut 48 doubled 13 cm length of linen thread. Fold in half and draw ends through the loop with a crochet hook and tighten. Use doubled thread for each knot.

RED ROSE AND YELLOW ROSE PILLOWS   shown on page 1

MATERIALS

Fabric: Beige silk, 41 cm square. Moss green velveteen, 90 cm by 73 cm.

Threads: D.M.C. # 25 six-strand embroidery floss.
FOR RED ROSE PILLOW
1 skein each of 814, 815, 816, 498, 304 (scarlet), 321 (turkey red), 817, 349, 350, 351 (geranium red), 319, 320, 367, 368 (pistachio green), 986, 987, 988, 989 (laurel green), 813, 825, 826, 827 (forget-me-not blue), 518, 519 (sky blue), 913, 954 and 955 (emerald green). Small amount each of 902 (scarlet), 356 (terra-cotta), 326 (garnet red), 517 (sky blue) and 347 (cardinal red).
FOR YELLOW ROSE PILLOW
1 skein each of 608 (flame red), 947 (fire red), 741, 742, 743, 744, 745 (tangerine yellow), 937, 469, 470, 471, 472, (moss green), 3347, 3348 (scarab green), 731, 732 (yellow green) and white. Small amount each of 444 (buttercup yellow), 307, 445 (lemon yellow), 3328, 760, 761 (morocco red), 3046 (beige),

740 (tangerine yellow) and 435 (umber).
Olive braid, 1.2 cm by 140 cm. One zipper, 32 cm long. Inner pillow stuffed with 600 grams of kapok.

FINISHED SIZE: See diagram.

DIRECTIONS: Cut fabric as indicated (see diagram). Trace actual size pattern. Transfer design to fabric. Reverse arrangement for yellow rose pillow. Work all embroidery in long and short stitch with two strands of floss in needle unless otherwise indicated. Press, When embroidery is finished. Sew zipper in place. Join three strips of velveteen together to form a complete circle. Turn to right side, fold in half lengthwise. Run a gathering stitch 1 cm from folded edge. Pull up bobbin threads and adjust gathers evenly. With right sides of embroidered piece and back piece facing, and ruffle between, stitch around four sides. Turn inside out. Insert inner pillow. Slip stitch braid along edges overcasting ends.

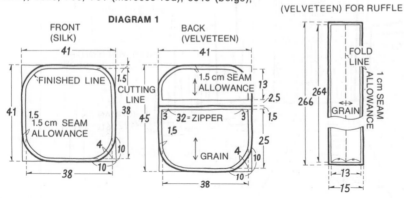

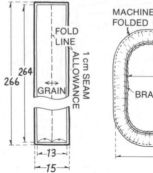

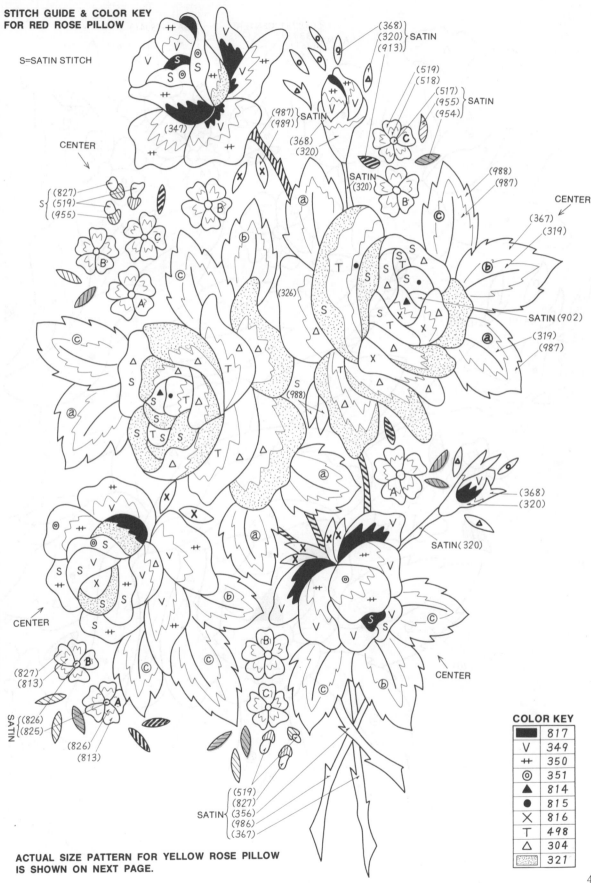

STITCH GUIDE & COLOR KEY
FOR RED ROSE PILLOW

S=SATIN STITCH

(368)
(320) } SATIN
(913)

(987)
(989) } SATIN

(519)
(518) } SATIN

(517)
(955) } SATIN
(954)

(347)

CENTER

(827)
S { (519)
(955)

(988)
(987)

CENTER

(367)
(319)

(368)
(320) } SATIN

(326)

SATIN (902)

(319)
(987)

(988)

S
(988)

(368)
(320)

SATIN (320)

CENTER

(827)
(813)

SATIN { (826)
(825)

(826)
(813)

CENTER

(519)
(827)
SATIN { (356)
(986)
(367)

ACTUAL SIZE PATTERN FOR YELLOW ROSE PILLOW
IS SHOWN ON NEXT PAGE.

COLOR KEY	
▰	817
V	349
++	350
◉	351
▲	814
●	815
×	816
T	498
△	304
▨	321

43

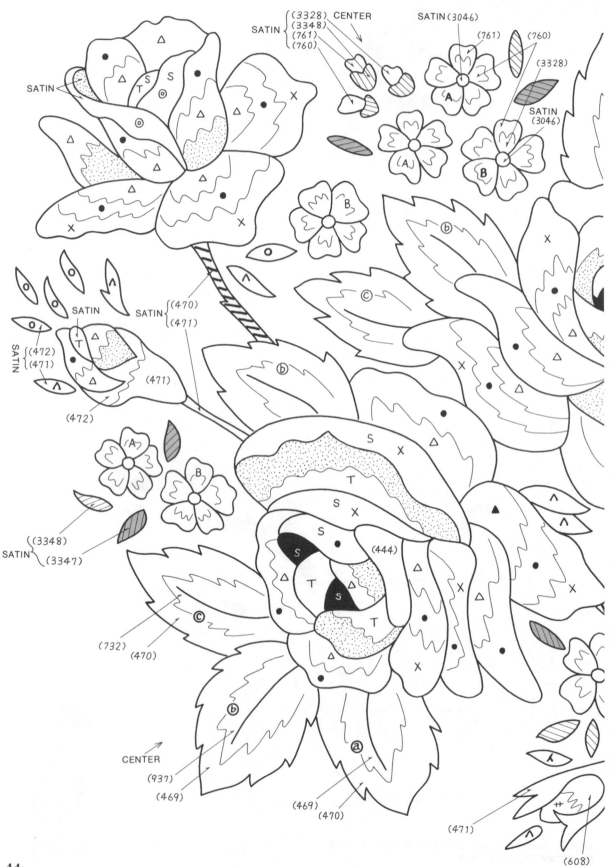

STITCH GUIDE AND COLOR KEY
FOR YELLOW ROSE PILLOW
S = SATIN STITCH

COLOR KEY

■	947
▲	307
⊢⊢	740
T	741
░	742
△	743
●	744
✕	745
◎	WHITE

CENTER

SATIN

SATIN
(471)

SATIN
(470)

(445)

(3347) } SATIN
(3348)

(761)
(760)
(3328) } SATIN
(435)
(469)
(731)

(471) } SATIN
(470)

(608) CENTER

45

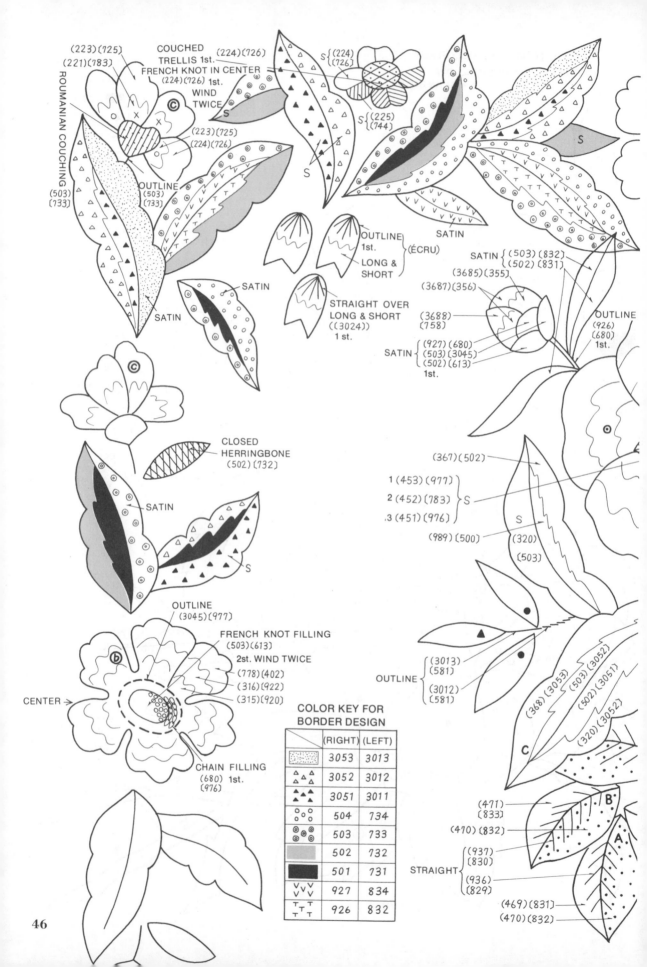

(223)(725)
(221)(783)
COUCHED TRELLIS 1st.
FRENCH KNOT IN CENTER
(224)(726) 1st.
WIND TWICE
(224)(726)
S {(224)(726)}
S {(225)(744)}
ROUMANIAN COUCHING
(503)(733)
(223)(725)
(224)(726)
OUTLINE (503)(733)
SATIN
SATIN
SATIN
S

OUTLINE 1st.
LONG & SHORT (ÉCRU)
STRAIGHT OVER LONG & SHORT ((3024)) 1st.

SATIN {(503)(832)}
      {(502)(831)}
(3685)(355)
(3687)(356)
(3688)(758)
SATIN {(927)(680)}
      {(503)(3045)}
      {(502)(613)} 1st.
OUTLINE (926)(680) 1st.

CLOSED HERRINGBONE (502)(732)
SATIN
S

(367)(502)
1 (453)(977)
2 (452)(783) } S
3 (451)(976)
(989)(500)
S
(320)
(503)

OUTLINE (3045)(977)
FRENCH KNOT FILLING (503)(613)
2st. WIND TWICE
(778)(402)
(316)(922)
(315)(920)
CENTER →
CHAIN FILLING (680) 1st. (976)

(3013)(581)
OUTLINE
(3012)(581)
(368)(3053) (503)(3052) (502)(3051)
(320)(3052)
C

(471)(833)
(470)(832)
STRAIGHT {(937)(830)}
         {(936)(829)}
(469)(831)
(470)(832)
B
A

COLOR KEY FOR BORDER DESIGN

46

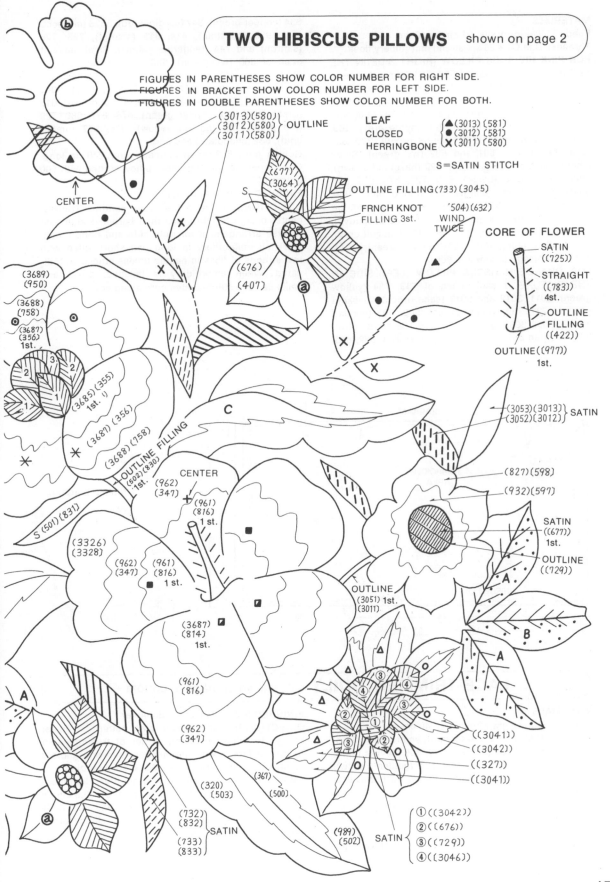

TWO HIBISCUS PILLOWS shown on page 2

FIGURES IN PARENTHESES SHOW COLOR NUMBER FOR RIGHT SIDE.
FIGURES IN BRACKET SHOW COLOR NUMBER FOR LEFT SIDE.
FIGURES IN DOUBLE PARENTHESES SHOW COLOR NUMBER FOR BOTH.

(3013)(580)
(3012)(580) } OUTLINE
(3011)(580)

LEAF
CLOSED
HERRINGBONE
▲(3013)(581)
●(3012)(581)
✗(3011)(580)

S=SATIN STITCH

CENTER

(677)
(3064)

S

OUTLINE FILLING(733)(3045)

FRNCH KNOT
FILLING 3st.

'504)(632)
WIND
TWICE

CORE OF FLOWER

SATIN
((725))

STRAIGHT
((783))
4st.

OUTLINE
FILLING
((422))

OUTLINE((977))
1st.

(676)
(407)

(3689)
(950)

(3688)
(758)

(3687)
(356)
1st.

2 3 2
1
1 2

(3685)(355)
1st.

(3687)(356)

(3688)(758)

OUTLINE FILLING
(502)(830)
1st.

CENTER

C

(3053)(3013)
(3052)(3012) SATIN

(827)(598)

(932)(597)

SATIN
((677))
1st.

OUTLINE
((729))

A

S(501)(831)

(3326)
(3328)

(962)
(347)

(962)
(347)

(961)
(816)
1st.

(961)
(816)
1st.

OUTLINE
(3051) 1st.
(3011)

B

A

(3687)
(814)
1st.

(961)
(816)

(962)
(347)

A

③
④

④

③

①
②

③
②

((3041))
((3042))
((327))
((3041))

(320)
(503)

(367)

(500)

(732)
(832)
SATIN
(733)
(833)

(989)
(502)

SATIN

①((3042))
②((676))
③((729))
④((3046))

47

MATERIALS

Fabric: Silver grey silk, 91 cm by 46 cm

Threads: D.M.C. #25 six-strand embroidery floss

FOR PINK HIBISCUS PILLOW (RIGHT SIDE IN THE PICTURE) 1 skein each of 503, 504 (almond green), 3051, 3052 and 3053 (green). ½ skein each of 3685, 3687, 3688, 3689 (raspberry red), 315, 316, 778 (dull mauve), 223, 224, 225 (faded pink), 961, 962 (magenta rose), 3326 (soft pink), 926, 927 (myrtle grey), 469, 470, 471 (moss green), 989 (laurel green), 320, 368 (pistachio green), 501 and 502 (ivy green). Small amount each of 725 (saffron), 422 (hazel-nut brown), 3024, 3045, 3046 (beige), 680, 729, 676, 677 (old gold), 783 (golden yellow), 221 (faded pink), 936, 937 (moss green), 367 (pistachio green), 932 (antique blue), 827 (forget-me-not blue), 327 (violet mauve), 3041, 3042 (Indian red), 451, 452, 453 (seagull grey), 977 (umber gold), 732, 733 (yellow green), 3011, 3012, 3013 (sage green) and écru.

FOR ORANGE HIBISCUS PILLOW (LEFT SIDE IN THE PICTURE) 1 skein each of 733, 734 (yellow green), 3011, 3012 and 3013 (sage green). ½ skein each of 731, 732 (yellow green), 502, 503 (almond green), 3052, 3053 (green), 355, 356, 758 (terra-cotta), 920, 922 (red brown), 402 (mahogany), 831, 832, 833, 834 (copper green), 347 (cardinal red), 3328 (morocco red), 950 (chestnut), 814, 816 (scarlet), 725, 726 (saffron) and 744 (tangerine yellow). Small amount each of 500 (ivy green), 580, 581 (golden green), 3051 (green), 597, 598 (greenish grey), 407 (chestnut), 3046 (brown), 3024, 327 (violet mauve), 3041, 3042 (Indian red), 3045 (beige), 422 (hazel-nut brown), 613 (drab), 829, 830 (copper green), 676, 677, 680, 729 (old gold), 783 (golden yellow), 976, 977 (umber gold), 632 (chocolate) and écru.

Golden cord, 0.8 cm in diameter and 270 cm long. One zipper, 38 cm long. Inner pillow stuffed with 500 grams of kapok.

FINISHED SIZE: 44 cm square.

DIRECTIONS: Trace actual size pattern. Transfer center design to fabric and then border design with reverse arrangement for right side and bottom half. Work all embroidery in long and short stitch with two strands of floss in needle unless otherwise indicated. When embroidery is finished, press and make up. Slip stitch golden cord along edges.

DIAGRAM

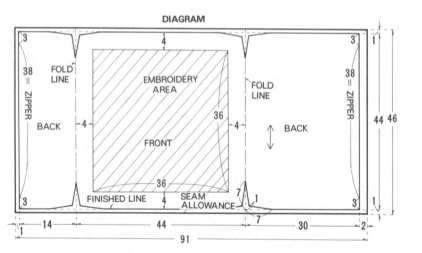

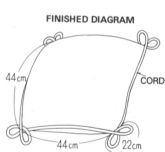

FINISHED DIAGRAM

LACE-TRIMMED DOILY shown on page 3, bottom

MATERIALS

Fabric: Light-weight white linen, 40 cm square.

Threads: D.M.C. #25 six-strand embroidery floss. 1 skein each of 334 (indigo), 799, 800 (Sèvres blue), 809 (forget-me-not blue), 580, 581 (golden yellow), 471, 472 (moss green), 3325, 775 (azure blue), 913, 954, 955 (emerald green), 991, 992 and 993 (peacock green). Small amount each of 368 (pistachio green), 597, 598 (greenish grey), 733 (yellow green), 470, 966 (moss green), 989 (laurel green), 744 (tangerine yellow), 806, 807 (peacock blue) and 813 (forget-me-not blue).

White lace, 1.5 cm by 110 cm.

FINISHED SIZE: 34.5 cm in diameter.

DIRECTIONS: Trace actual size pattern. Transfer design to fabric matching center of tracing paper to that of fabric, with one section following another to make a complete circle. Work all embroidery in satin stitch with one strand of floss in needle unless otherwise indicated. Cut out circle of 33.5 cm in diameter. Slip stitch around edge with 0.3 cm double hem. Place white lace 0.3 cm deep along folded edge. Slip stitch. Press.

FINISHED DIAGRAM

32 cm

FINISHED LINE OF FABRIC

345 cm

LACE 1.5 cm WIDE

CENTER

A = (800)
B = (809)
C = (799)
D = (334)
E = (3325)
F = (775)

OUTLINE (581)

(581)

(913)

(954)

(955)

(470)

OUTLINE (470)

(733)

(806)

(807)

CLOSED HERRINGBONE (580) 2st.

CENTER

FRENCH KNOT FILLING (744) 2st.

(471)

(472)

(471)

OUTLINE (472)

(472)

(991)

(993)

(992)

(966)

(813)

(3325)

(368)

OUTLINE (989) (368)

OUTLINE (989)

(989)

OUTLINE (368)

(598)

(597)

FINISHED LINE

OUTLINE (471)

OUTLINE (472)

(472)

16 cm

49

SCALLOPED DOILY   shown on page 3, top

MATERIALS

Fabric: Light-weight light green linen, 40 cm square.
Threads: D.M.C. #25 six-strand embroidery floss.
2 skeins each of 347 (cardinal red) and 760 (morocco red). 1 skein each of 470, 471 (moss green), 598 (greenish grey), white and écru. ½ skein each of 725 (saffron) and 744 (tangerine yellow).
FINISHED SIZE: 36.5 cm in diameter
DIRECTIONS: Trace actual size pattern. Transfer design to fabric matching center of tracing paper to that of fabric with one section following another to make a complete circle. Work all embroidery in satin stitch with two strands of floss in needle unless otherwise indicated. Buttonhole stitch along scallop outline. Trim fabric beyond stitching. Press.

CENTER

ONE EIGHTH PATTERN

45°

FINISHED DIAGRAM

36,5

18,2   15,2

SHADOW (WHITE)

LONG & SHORT
(760)
(347)

(470)

OUTLINE

OUTLINE
FILLING
(ÉCRU)

(744)

(725)

OUTLINE
(471)

(471)

BUTTONHOLE SCALLOP

BUTTONHOLE SCALLOP
(598)

THREE ROSES WITH BUDS PILLOW   shown on page 4

MATERIALS

Fabric: Silver grey silk, 92 cm by 44 cm
Threads: D.M.C. #25 six-strand embroidery floss
1 skein each of 350, 351, 352 (geranium red), 742, 743, 744 (tangerine yellow), 972 (canary yellow), 469, 471 (moss green), 581 (golden green), 988 (laurel green), 3346, 3347 (scarab green), 904, 905, 906 (parakeet green) and 435 (umber). Small amount each of 353, 349, 754, 817, 948 (geranium red), 761 (morocco red), 321 (turkey red), 891 (geranium pink), 606, 608 (flame red), 741, 745 (tangerine yellow), 726, 727 (saffron), 907, 971 (canary yellow), 320, 368

(pistachio green), 470, 472 (moss green), 975 (umber gold) and 989 (laurel green).

Grey cord, 0.5 cm in diameter and 220 cm long. One zipper, 38 cm long. Inner pillow stuffed with 400 grams of kapok.

FINISHED SIZE: See diagram.

DIRECTIONS: Cut fabric as indicated (see diagram). Trace actual size pattern and transfer design to fabric. Reverse arrangement for sprigs around the center design (see diagram). Work all embroidery in long and short stitch with two strands of floss in needle unless otherwise indicated. When embroidery is finished, press and make up. Slip stitch grey cord along four sides.

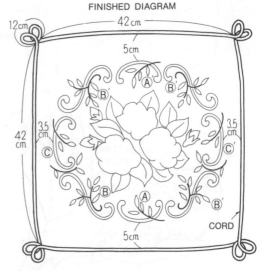

FINISHED DIAGRAM

A' B' AND C' ARE REVERSED PATTERNS OF A, B AND C RESPECTIVELY.

51

S=SATIN STITCH

52

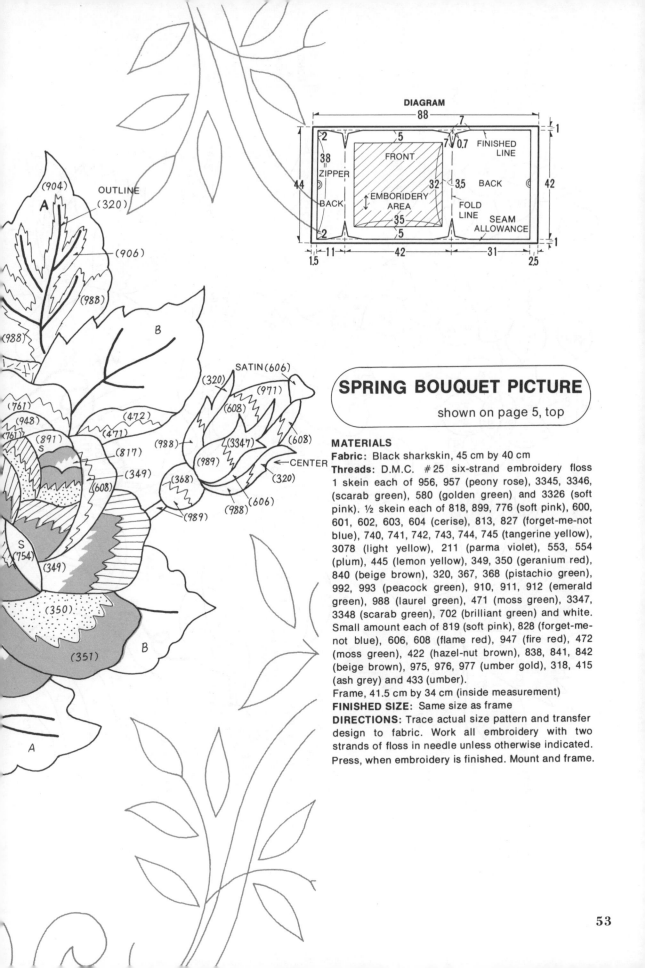

DIAGRAM

(labels within diagram:)
88
7
2
5
7 0.7 FINISHED LINE
38 FRONT
ZIPPER
44 32 3.5 BACK
BACK
EMBROIDERY AREA
FOLD LINE
35 SEAM ALLOWANCE
2 5
42
11 42 31
1.5 2.5
1
1
42

OUTLINE (320)

(904)
A
(906)
(988)
(988)
B
(761)
(948)
(761)
(891)
S
(817)
(349)
(608)
S
(754)
(349)
(350)
(351)
B
A

SATIN (606)
(320)
(971)
(608)
(988)
(3347)
(608)
(989)
CENTER
(320)
(368)
(989)
(988) (606)

SPRING BOUQUET PICTURE

shown on page 5, top

MATERIALS

Fabric: Black sharkskin, 45 cm by 40 cm

Threads: D.M.C. #25 six-strand embroidery floss 1 skein each of 956, 957 (peony rose), 3345, 3346, (scarab green), 580 (golden green) and 3326 (soft pink). ½ skein each of 818, 899, 776 (soft pink), 600, 601, 602, 603, 604 (cerise), 813, 827 (forget-me-not blue), 740, 741, 742, 743, 744, 745 (tangerine yellow), 3078 (light yellow), 211 (parma violet), 553, 554 (plum), 445 (lemon yellow), 349, 350 (geranium red), 840 (beige brown), 320, 367, 368 (pistachio green), 992, 993 (peacock green), 910, 911, 912 (emerald green), 988 (laurel green), 471 (moss green), 3347, 3348 (scarab green), 702 (brilliant green) and white. Small amount each of 819 (soft pink), 828 (forget-me-not blue), 606, 608 (flame red), 947 (fire red), 472 (moss green), 422 (hazel-nut brown), 838, 841, 842 (beige brown), 975, 976, 977 (umber gold), 318, 415 (ash grey) and 433 (umber).

Frame, 41.5 cm by 34 cm (inside measurement)

FINISHED SIZE: Same size as frame

DIRECTIONS: Trace actual size pattern and transfer design to fabric. Work all embroidery with two strands of floss in needle unless otherwise indicated. Press, when embroidery is finished. Mount and frame.

53

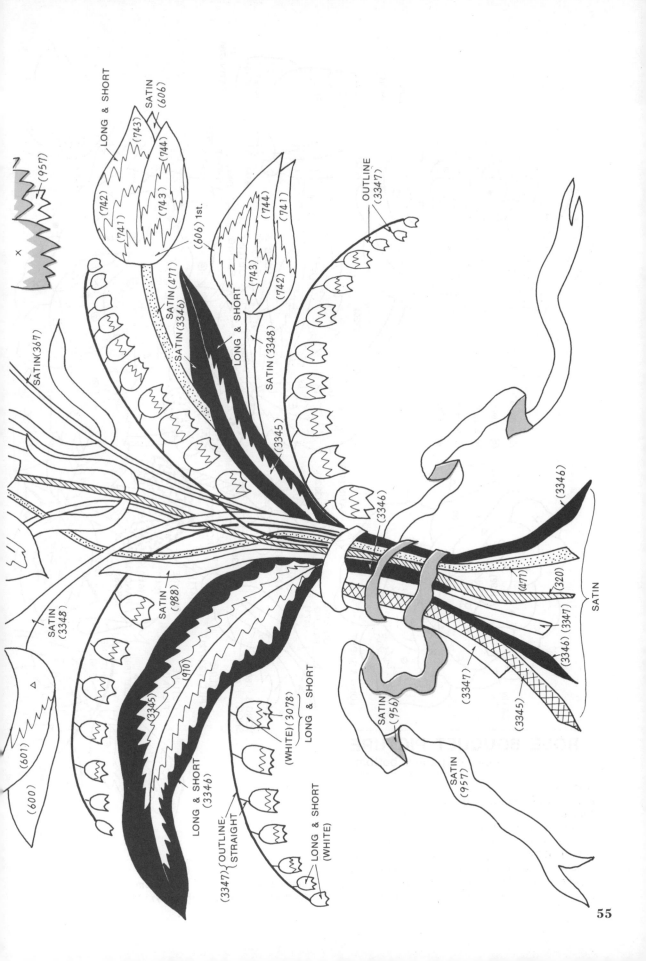

LONG & SHORT

SATIN (606)

(957)

×

(743)

(744)

(742)

(741)

(743)

(741)

SATIN (361)

(606) 1st.

SATIN (471)

SATIN (3346)

(744)

(741)

(743)

(742)

LONG & SHORT

SATIN (3348)

OUTLINE (3347)

(3345)

(3346)

SATIN (988)

SATIN (3348)

(910)

(600)

(601)

△

(3345)

(3346)

(477)

(320)

SATIN

(3346) (3347)

(3345)

(3347)

SATIN (956)

SATIN (957)

(WHITE) (3078)

LONG & SHORT

LONG & SHORT (3346)

(3347) OUTLINE, STRAIGHT

LONG & SHORT (WHITE)

55

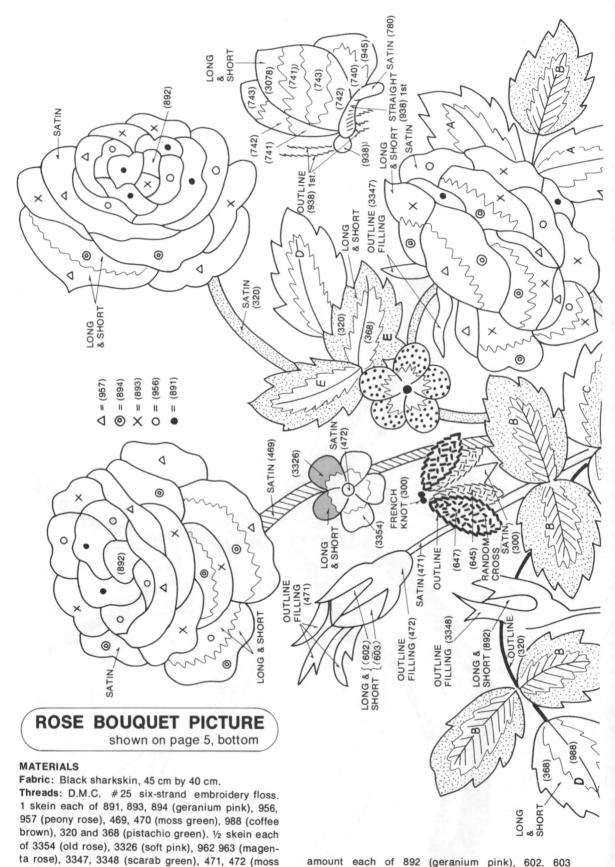

SATIN

(892)

LONG & SHORT

LONG & SHORT STRAIGHT SATIN (780)

(3078) (741) (743) (742) (740) (945)
(743)
(742)
(741)

OUTLINE (938) 1st.

(938)

(938)

LONG & SHORT

SATIN (938) 1st

OUTLINE (3347)

A

A

LONG & SHORT

OUTLINE FILLING

LONG & SHORT

SATIN (320)

D

(320)

(368)

E

E

C

SATIN (469)

(3326)

SATIN (472)

B

△ = (957)
◎ = (894)
✕ = (893)
○ = (956)
● = (891)

FRENCH KNOT (300)

RANDOM CROSS

(647)

(645)

SATIN (300)

(892)

LONG & SHORT

(3354)

LONG & SHORT

SATIN

LONG & SHORT

OUTLINE FILLING (471)

OUTLINE FILLING (472)

SATIN (471)

OUTLINE (3348)

OUTLINE (320)

B

LONG & SHORT (892)

LONG & { (602)
& { (603)
SHORT

B

(988)

B

D

(368)

LONG & SHORT

ROSE BOUQUET PICTURE
shown on page 5, bottom

MATERIALS

Fabric: Black sharkskin, 45 cm by 40 cm.
Threads: D.M.C. #25 six-strand embroidery floss.
1 skein each of 891, 893, 894 (geranium pink), 956, 957 (peony rose), 469, 470 (moss green), 988 (coffee brown), 320 and 368 (pistachio green). ½ skein each of 3354 (old rose), 3326 (soft pink), 962 963 (magenta rose), 3347, 3348 (scarab green), 471, 472 (moss green), 991, 992 and 993 (peacock green). Small

amount each of 892 (geranium pink), 602, 603 (cerise), 300, 402, (mahogany), 741, 742 (tangerine

(3326)
(3354)
(3326)
(3354)
LONG & SHORT (963)
SATIN (962)
LONG & SHORT
LONG & SHORT
SATIN (320)
OUTLINE (320)
LONG & SHORT (963)
LONG & SHORT (962)
(3354)
LONG & SHORT
SATIN (988)
LONG & SHORT
(320)
(469)
B
LONG & SHORT
(320) (368)
SATIN (911)
OUTLINE (402)
SATIN (320)
(963)
SATIN (471)
SATIN (472)
(469)
(470)
C
C
C
OUTLINE (469)
SATIN (402)
C
(469)
(469)
SATIN (469)
(470)
SATIN (992)
(471)
SATIN (993)
SATIN
(892)
A
(470)
(471)
(471)
SATIN (470)
OUTLINE (469)
A
LONG & SHORT (988) (470)
LONG & SHORT
LONG & SHORT
LONG & SHORT
OUTLINE FILLING
(3347)
SATIN (892)
SATIN (3348)
(893)

yellow), 945 (apricot pink), 938 (coffee brown), 780
(golden yellow), 645 and 647 (beaver grey).
Frame, 41.5 cm by 34 cm (inside measurement).
FINISHED SIZE: Same size as frame.
DIRECTIONS: Trace actual size pattern and transfer
design to fabric. Work all embroidery with two strands
of floss in needle unless otherwise indicated. Press,
when embroidery is finished. Mount and frame.

TABLE CENTER AND PLACE MATS shown on page 6

DIAGRAM

TABLE CENTER

PLACE MAT

MATERIALS

Fabric: Yellow linen, 45 cm by 130 cm for table center. Yellow linen, 55 cm by 40 cm for one place mat.

Threads: D.M.C. # 25 six-strand embroidery floos.

FOR TABLE CENTER

1 sekin each of 550 (plum), 327 (violet mauve), 3042 (Indian red), 335 (garnet red), 776, 899 (soft pink), 3688, 3689 (raspberry red), 963 (magenta rose), 347 (cardinal red), 760 (morocco red), 991 (peakcock green), 320, 367 (pistachio green), 913 (emerald green) and 966 (moss green). ½ sekin each of 350 (geranium red), 920, 921 (red brown), 831, 832, 833, 834 (copper green), 732 (yellow green), 368 and 369 (pistachio green). Small amount each of 972 (canary yellow), 74¹ 743 (tangerine yellow), 945 (apricot pink), 922 (red brown), 402 (mahogany), 977 (umber gold), 783 (golden yellow), 734 (yellow green), 3047, 3024 (beige) and 367 (pistachio green).

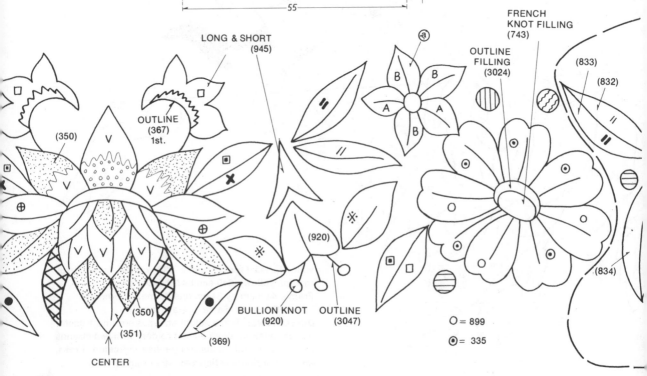

LONG & SHORT (945)

OUTLINE (367) 1st.

(350)

(350)

(351)

CENTER

(369)

BULLION KNOT (920)

OUTLINE (3047)

(920)

FRENCH KNOT FILLING (743)

OUTLINE FILLING (3024)

(833)

(832)

(834)

○ = 899

◉ = 335

FOR ONE PLACE MAT

½ skein each of 550 (plum), 327 (violet mauve), 3042 (Indian red), 3688, 3689 (raspberry red), 776 (soft pink), 963 (magenta rose), 326 (garnet red), 347 (cardinal red), 350, 351 (geranium red), 760 (morocco red), 832, 833, 834 (copper green), 991 (peacock green), 320, 367 (pistachio green), 913 (emerald green) and 966 (moss green). Small amount each of 972 (canary yellow), 741 (tangerine yellow), 945 (apricot pink), 922 (red brown), 402 (mahogany), 977 (umber gold), 783 (golden yellow), and 3024 (beige).

FINISHED SIZE: Table center, 38 cm by 123 cm. Place mat, 35 cm by 50 cm.

DIRECTIONS: Trace actual size pattern. For place mat, use pattern in the dotted line. Transfer design to fabric reversing arrangement for left side and top half. Work in satin stitch with two strands of floss in needle unless otherwise indicated. Pull out four threads of fabric, 4 cm from place mat edges and 5.5 cm from table center edges. Fold edges 1 cm all around to back for place mat, 1.5 cm for table center. Refold hem and hem stitch inner edges to pulled thread line, mitering corners neatly. Press.

CLOSED HERRINGBONE (991)

CLOSED HERRINGBONE

CLOSED HERRINGBONE CENTER

(913)
(760)
(351)
(351)
(351)
(350)
(351) (760)

OUTLINE FILLING (783)

LONG & SHORT { (349) (347)

(977)

OUTLINE (966)
(922)

C
D
D
D
C
B
A
B
B
A

T
T

□
▣

D
C
D
D
C

(3024)
(3689)
(3688)

(550)
(741)
(945)
(402)
(913)
(320)

(327)
(3024)
(963)
(776)

(3042)
(972)

B
B
A
A
B

OUTLINE (783)

LONG & SHORT (367)

(832) (834)
LONG & SHORT

OUTLINE (367) 1st.

□ = (367)
▣ = (320)
✖ = (368)
V = (349)
✳ = (921)
T = (966)
⊕ = (350)

ANEMONE WAGON MAT   shown on page 9

MATERIALS

Fabric: Light-weight white linen, 57 cm by 42 cm.
Threads: D.M.C. #25 six-strand embroidery floss.
1½ skeins each of 309 (garnet red) and 988 (laurel green). 1 skein each of 987, 989 (laurel green), 320, 368 (pistachio green), 912, 913, 954, 955 (emerald green), 992 (peacock green), 326, 335 (garnet red), 899 (soft pink), 208, 209, 210 (parma violet), 414, 415, 762 (ash grey) and 518 (sky blue). Small amount each of 211 (parma violet), 740, 741, 743, 744, 745 (tangerine yellow), 317, 318, 413 (ash grey), 801,

938 (coffee brown) and 977 (umber gold). White sewing thread #60.

FINISHED SIZE: 53 cm by 38 cm.

DIRECTIONS: Trace actual size pattern. Transfer design to fabric, reversing arrangement for right side and top half (see diagram). Work in long and short stitch with two strands of floss in needle unless otherwise indicated. Pull out four threads of fabric, 3.5 cm from edges. Fold edges 0.5 cm all around to back and refold 1.5 cm. Hem stitch with white sewing thread. Press.

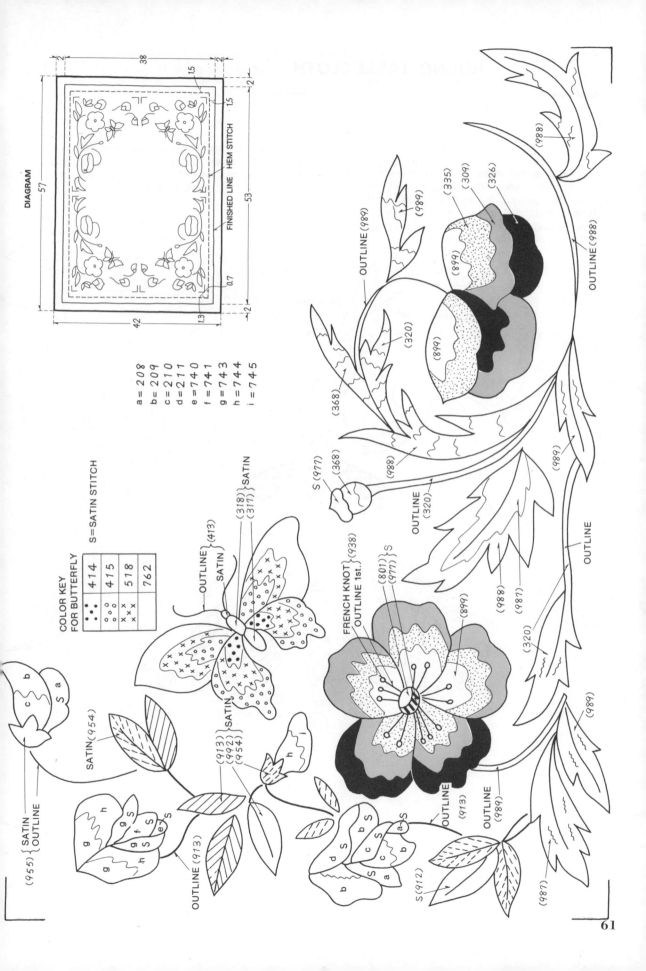

DIAGRAM

FINISHED LINE   HEM STITCH

38
57
53
42
2
2
1.5
1.5
0.7
1.3
2

a = 208
b = 209
c = 210
d = 211
e = 740
f = 741
g = 743
h = 744
i = 745

COLOR KEY
FOR BUTTERFLY

	414
°°°	415
××× ×××	518
	762

S = SATIN STITCH

OUTLINE } SATIN (413)

(318) (317) } SATIN

SATIN (954)

(913) (992) (954) } SATIN

OUTLINE (913)

(955) { SATIN OUTLINE

OUTLINE (413)

FRENCH KNOT } (938) OUTLINE 1st. }

(801) (977) } S

OUTLINE (989)

(335)
(309)
(326)

(899)

(899)

(988)
(989)

(320)

(899)

(368)

OUTLINE (988)

S (977)
(368)
(988)

OUTLINE (320)

(989)

OUTLINE

(988)
(987)

(320)

OUTLINE

(899)

OUTLINE (913)

OUTLINE (989)

(989)

S (912)

(987)

b
c
S   a

g
h
g S
g f S
g h S e S
g

d S
c S
b S
a S
a-S
b
b

S (912)

h
i

61

MATERIALS

Fabric: Light brown linen, 180 cm square.
Threads: D.M.C. # 25 six-strand embroidery floss.
3 skeins each of 355 (garnet red), 3053 (green) and
613 (drab). 2 skeins each of 611, 612 (drab), 3011,
3012, 3013 (sage green), 3051, 3052 (green), 3064
(brown) and 407 (chestnut). 1 skein each of 829,
831 (copper green), 680, 729 (old gold), 869, 420
(hazel-nut brown), 783 (golden yellow), 975, 976
(umber gold), 632 (chocolate), 840 (beige brown)
and 725 (saffron). Small amount of 642 (smoke grey).
FINISHED SIZE: 160 cm in diameter.

DIRECTIONS: Trace actual size pattern. Transfer
design to fabric, reversing pattern alternately to
make a circle (see diagram). Work with two strands
of floss in needle unless otherwise indicated. When
embroidery is finished, cut out circle of 160 cm in
diameter. Cut several strips on the bias from scraps
of fabric and join them to make binding of 3 cm by

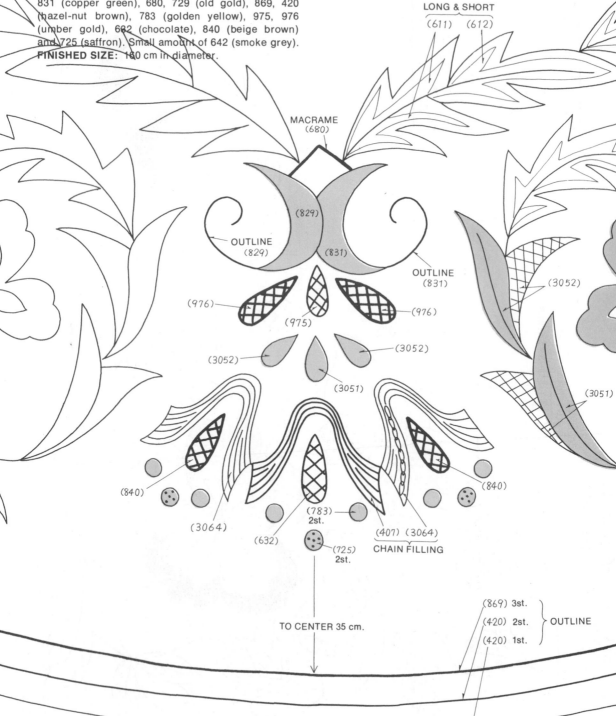

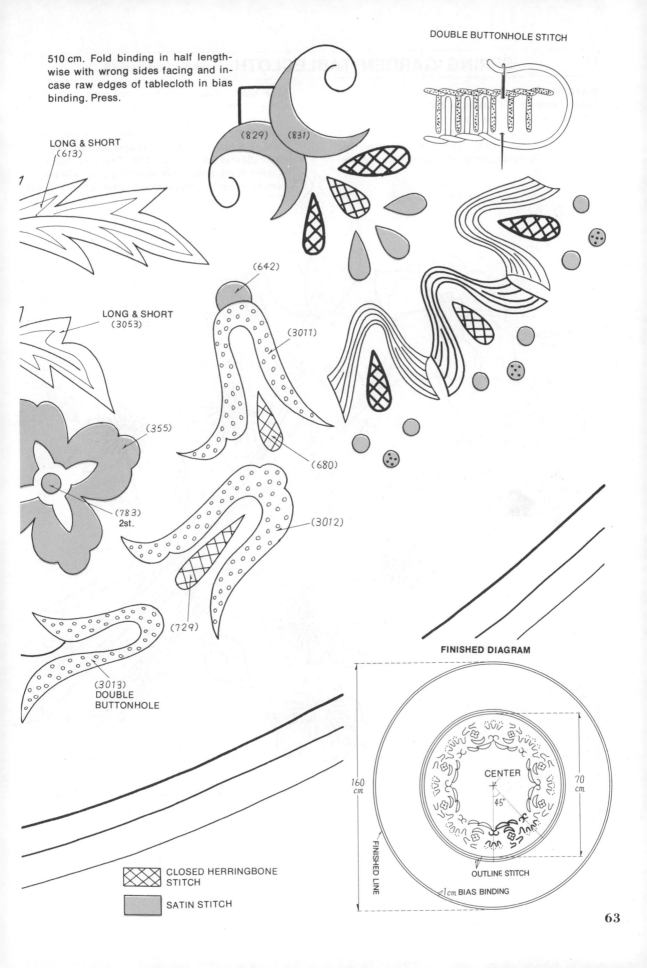

DOUBLE BUTTONHOLE STITCH

510 cm. Fold binding in half lengthwise with wrong sides facing and incase raw edges of tablecloth in bias
binding. Press.

LONG & SHORT
(613)

(829) (831)

LONG & SHORT
(3053)

(642)

(3011)

(355)

(680)

(783)
2st.

(3012)

(729)

(3013)
DOUBLE
BUTTONHOLE

FINISHED DIAGRAM

160
cm

70
cm

CENTER

45°

FINISHED LINE

OUTLINE STITCH

1 cm BIAS BINDING

⬚ CLOSED HERRINGBONE
STITCH

▢ SATIN STITCH

SPRING GARDEN TABLECLOTH shown on page 8

MATERIALS

Fabric: White linen, 126 cm by 166 cm.
Threads: D.M.C. # 25 six-strand embroidery floss.
3 skeins of 813 (forget-me-not blue). 2 skeins each
of 899, 3326 (soft pink), 320, 368, 369 (pistachio
green), 3347 (scarab green), 809 and 827 (forget-me-

not blue). 1 skein each of 208, 209, 210 (parma
violet), 601, 602, 603, 604, 605 (cerise), 741, 742,
743, 744, 745 (tangerine yellow), 893, 894 (geranium
pink), 956, 957 (emerald green), 776 (soft pink),
309, 335 (garnet red), 826 (forget-me-not blue), 799,
800 (Sévres blue), 517, 518, 519 (sky blue), 775
(azure blue), 3346, 3348 (scarab green), 470 and 471
(moss green). Small amount each of 211 (parma

COLOR KEY

MARK	COLOR NO.	MARK	COLOR NO.	MARK	COLOR NO.	MARK	COLOR NO.	MARK	COLOR NO.
A	601	K	956	U	335	e	517	w	3348
B	602	L	957	V	309	f	518	p	801
C	603	M	893	W	800	g	519	s	498
D	604	N	894	X	775	h	368	r	813
E	605	O	809	Y	818	i	369	x	827
F	741	P	799	Z	740	j	320	u	826
G	742	Q	725	a	208	k	470		
H	743	R	776	b	209	l	471		
I	744	S	3326	v	210	m	3346		
J	745	T	899	d	211	n	3347		

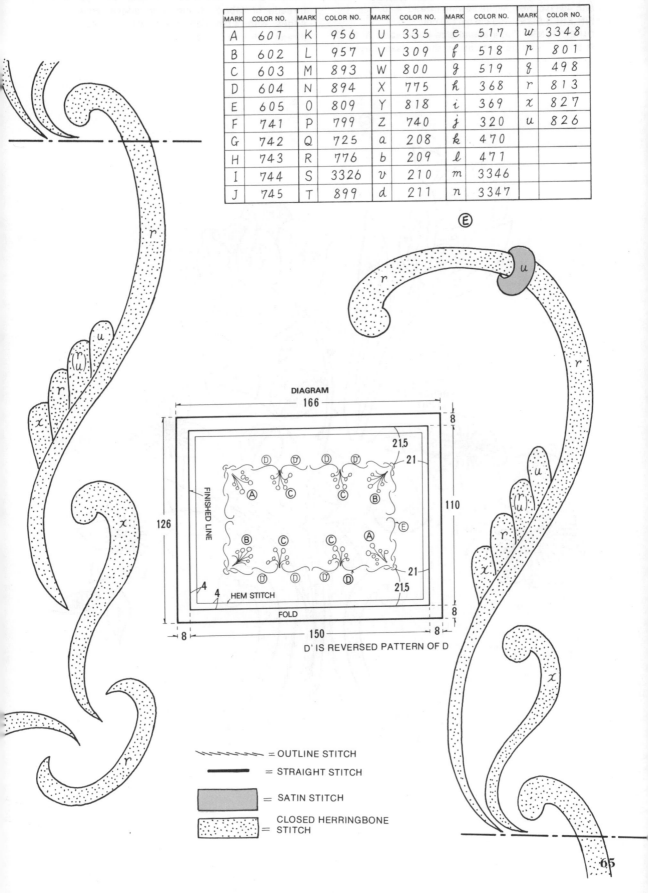

DIAGRAM

166

8

21.5

21

110

126

FINISHED LINE

21

21.5

8

4

4   HEM STITCH

FOLD

8   150   8

D' IS REVERSED PATTERN OF D

〰〰〰 = OUTLINE STITCH

▬▬▬ = STRAIGHT STITCH

▬ = SATIN STITCH

▒ = CLOSED HERRINGBONE STITCH

violet), 740 (tangerine yellow), 801 (coffee brown) and 498 (scarlet). White sewing thread #50.

FINISHED SIZE: 150 cm by 110 cm.

DIRECTIONS: Trace actual size patterns of A, B, C, D and E. Arrange patterns as shown (see diagram). Transfer design to fabric. Work all embroidery in long and short stitch with two strands of floss in needle unless otherwise indicated. Pull out three threads of fabric, 12 cm from edges. Hem stitch edges with 4 cm deep hem using white sewing thread, mitering corners neatly. Press.

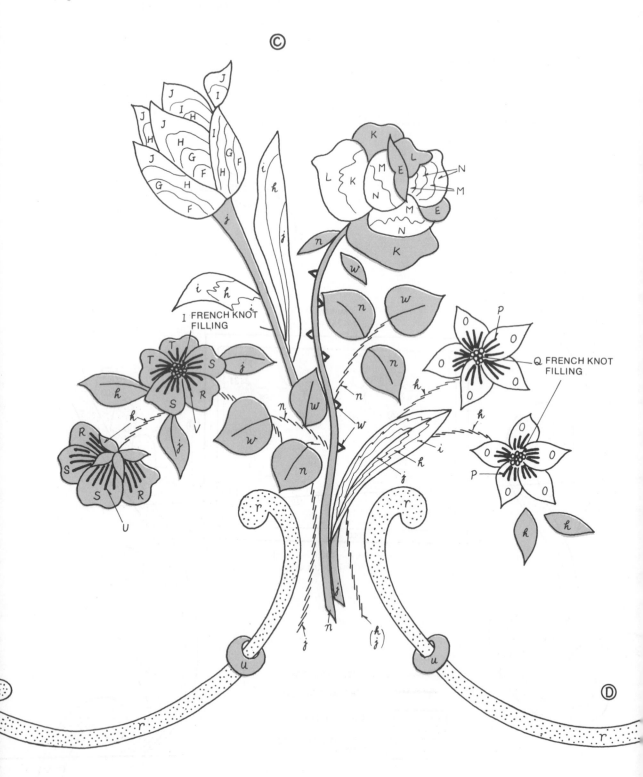

66

PILLOW shown on page 12

(992) (993)
OUTLINE
FILLING

OUTLINE
(911)
ⓑ

CLOSED
HERRINGBONE { (911)
(444)

OUTLINE
(742)

{ (911) } OUTLINE
{ (912) } ⓐ

(704) ▲

(307)

(704)

(954)

OUTLINE
(954)

ⓒ
(701)
(911)

(702)

(701)
○

(703)

(833)

OUTLINE
(993)

(831)

(993)

(992)

(597)

RANDOM
CROSS

(444)

(700)

(807)
(806)

(807)
(806)
(824)

(824)

(703)

(833)

ⓑ

OUTLINE
(701)

(702)

(700)

ⓐ

(912)

RANDOM
CROSS

(954)

(911)

OUTLINE
(911)

ⓒ

▲

◉

(996) (995)

LONG &
SHORT

(444)

CENTER

(704)

MATERIALS

Fabric: Beige shantung, 90 cm by 48 cm.
Threads: D.M.C. #25 six-strand embroidery floss.
2 skeins each of 993 (peacock green), and 703 (brilliant green). 1½ skeins of 992 (peacock green).
1 skein each of 700, 701, 702, 704 (brilliant green),
911, 912, 914 (emerald green) and 833 (copper
green). Small amount each of 597 (greenish grey),
824 (forget-me-not blue), 806, 807 (peacock green),
995, 996 (royal blue), 742 (tangerine yellow), 444
(buttercup yellow), 307 (lemon yellow) and 831
(copper green). Inner pillow stuffed with 550 grams
of kapok. Beige bias binding, 175 cm long. One zipper, 39 cm long.
FINISHED SIZE: 43 cm square.
DIRECTIONS: Cut fabric as indicated (see diagram).
Trace actual size pattern. Transfer design to fabric,
reversing arrangement for right side and bottom
half. Use two strands of floss in needle except random stitch which is worked with one strand of floss.
Work all embroidery in satin stitch unless otherwise
indicated. Sew zipper to back piece. Fold bias binding in half lengthwise. With right sides together,
insert bias binding between marking seam line 0.3
cm from folded edge, sew around edges with 1 cm
seams. Press. Turn right side out. Insert inner pillow.

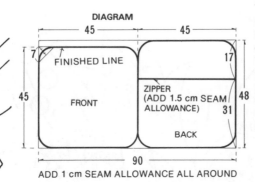

DIAGRAM

ADD 1 cm SEAM ALLOWANCE ALL AROUND

PIANO COVER   shown on pages 10–11

MATERIALS

Fabric: White linen, 90 cm by 200 cm.
Threads: D.M.C. #25 six-strand embroidery floss.
3 skeins each of 676 (old gold) and 3688
(raspberry red). 2 skeins each of 209 (parma
violet), 470 (moss green) and 3687 (raspberry red). 1 skein each of 208, 210 (parma
violet), 350, 351 (geranium red), 988, 989
(laurel green), 469, 471 (moss green), 741,
742 (tangerine yellow), 957 (peony rose),
963 (magenta rose), 782, 783 (golden yellow), 931 and 932 (antique blue). ½ skein
each of 211 (parma violet), 603 (cerise), 718
(episcopal purple), 743 (tangerine yellow),
472 (moss green), 987 (laurel green), 992
(peacock green), 806 (peacock blue), 956
(peony rose) and 3689 (raspberry red).
Small amount each of 349, 817 (geranium
red) and 729 (old gold).
White lace, 2.2 cm by 400 cm.
FINISHED SIZE: 201.4 cm by 90.7 cm.
DIRECTIONS: Trace actual size pattern.
Transfer design to fabric as shown in
diagram. Work all embroidery in long and
short stitch with two strands of floss in
needle unless otherwise indicated. Turn
0.5 cm edges to right side and turn another
0.5 cm. Slip stitch in place. Make a 2.5 cm
pleat at each wedged corner. Place white
lace 0.5 cm deep along folded edges and
slip stitch. Press. Cut ten 9 cm length of
six stranded old golden threads, double
through loop and tie all threads together
3.5cm from each end. Make ten tassels and
attach them in place with three crocheted
chains each.

DIAGRAM

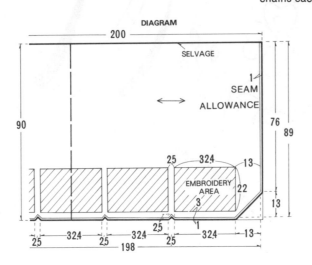

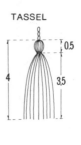

TASSEL

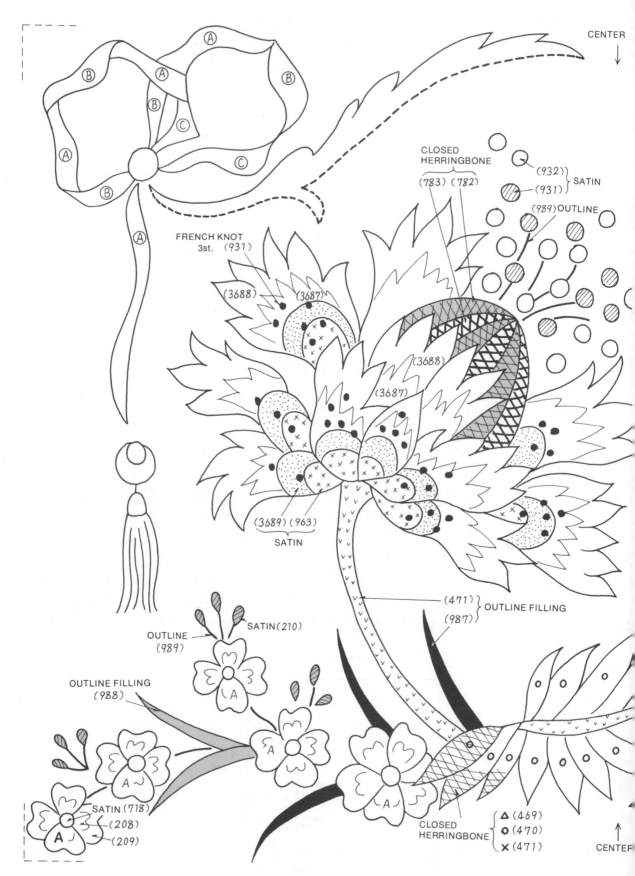

CENTER
↓

CLOSED
HERRINGBONE
(783) (782)

(932)
(931) ⎱ SATIN

(989) OUTLINE

FRENCH KNOT
3st. (931)

(3688)
(3687)

(3688)

(3687)

(3689) (963)
SATIN

OUTLINE
(989)

SATIN (210)

OUTLINE FILLING
(988)

(471) ⎱ OUTLINE FILLING
(987) ⎰

CLOSED
HERRINGBONE

△ (469)
○ (470)
✕ (471)

SATIN (718)
(208)
(209)

CENTER
↑

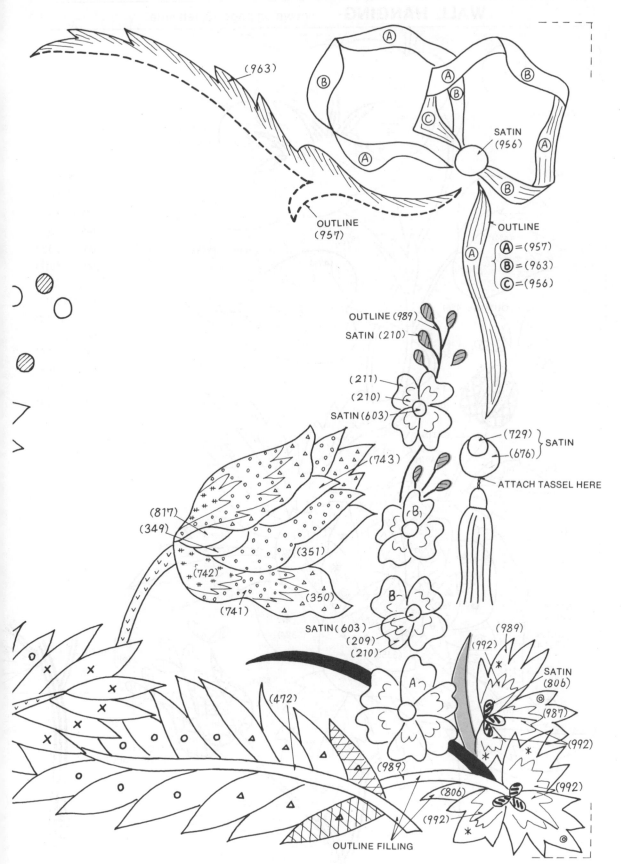

(963)

A

B

A
A
B

B

C

SATIN
(956)

A

A

B

OUTLINE
(957)

OUTLINE

A = (957)
B = (963)
C = (956)

OUTLINE (989)
SATIN (210)

(211)
(210)
SATIN (603)

(729)
(676) } SATIN

ATTACH TASSEL HERE

(743)

(817)
(349)

(351)

(742)

(350)
(741)

B

B

SATIN (603)
(209)
(210)

(989)
(992)

SATIN
(806)

(987)

(992)

(992)

(472)

A

(989)

OUTLINE FILLING

(806)

(992)

(992)

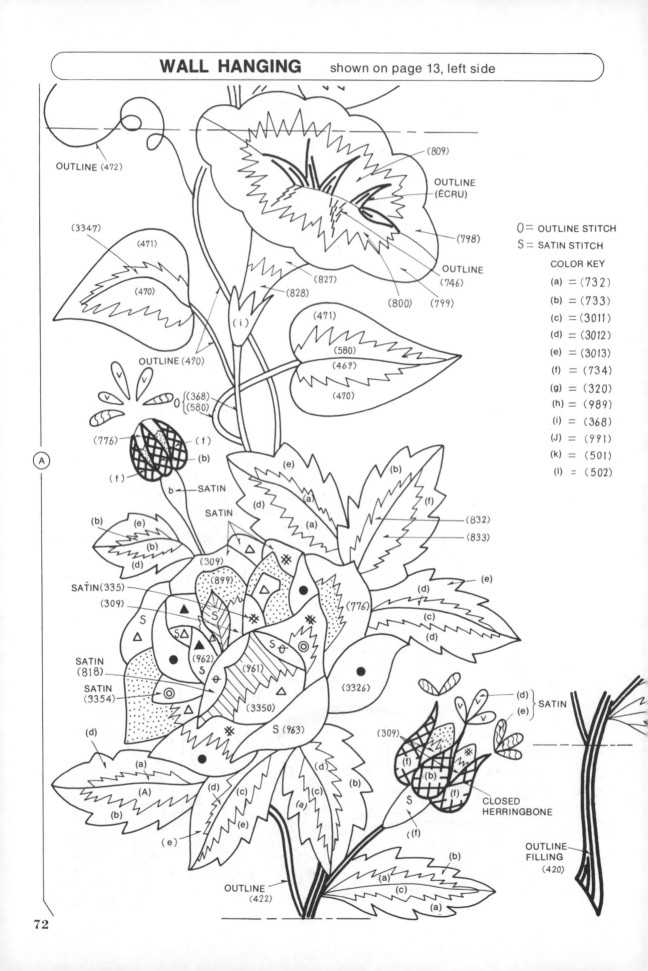

WALL HANGING shown on page 13, left side

OUTLINE (472)

(809)

OUTLINE (ÉCRU)

(798)

(3347)

(471)

(470)

(827)

(828)

OUTLINE (746)

(800)   (799)

(i)

(471)

(580)

(469)

(470)

OUTLINE (470)

0 { (368)
     (580)

(776)   (f)

(f)   (b)

(f)

b — SATIN

SATIN

(b)   (e)

(b)

(d)

(e)

(d)

(a)

(a)

(b)

(f)

(832)

(833)

(309)

(899)

SATIN (335)

(309)

(776)

(d)

(e)

S

△

(d)

(c)

S △

△

(d)

SATIN
(818)

● (962)

S

(961)

SATIN
(3354)

◎

(3350)

(3326)

(d)

(e) } SATIN

S (963)

(309)

(f)

(d)

(a)

(A)

(d)

(c)

(a)

(b)

(f)

(b)

(f)

CLOSED
HERRINGBONE

(b)

(e)

(d)

(c)

(e)

S

((f)

(b)

OUTLINE
FILLING
(420)

OUTLINE
(422)

(a)

(c)

(a)

O = OUTLINE STITCH
S = SATIN STITCH

COLOR KEY

(a) = (732)
(b) = (733)
(c) = (3011)
(d) = (3012)
(e) = (3013)
(f) = (734)
(g) = (320)
(h) = (989)
(i) = (368)
(J) = (991)
(k) = (501)
(l) = (502)

A

MATERIALS

Fabric: Pink silk, 82.5 cm by 18 cm. Pink cotton for lining, 82.5 cm by 14 cm.

Threads: D.M.C. # 25 six-strand embroidery floss. 1 skein each of 3685, 3687, 3688 (raspberry red), 3350, 3354 (old rose), 309, 335 (garnet red), 961, 962, 963 (magenta rose), 776, 818, 899, 3326 (soft pink), 798, 799, 800 (Sèvres blue), 809 (forget-me-not blue), 3011, 3012, 3013 (sage green), 732, 733, 734 (yellow green), 989 (laurel green), 580 (golden green), 3347 (scarab green), 469, 470, 471, 472 (moss green), 320, 368 (pistachio green), 501, 502 (ivy green), 832, 833 (copper green) and 991 (peacock green). Small amount each of 744 (tangerin yellow), 827, 828 (forget-me-not blue), 746 (cream), 3689 (raspberry red), 420, 422 (hazel-nut brown), 504 (almond green), 966 (moss green), 725 (saffron), 783 (golden yellow), 612 (drab) and écru.

One set of bell pull attachments. Iron-on interfacing, 78.5 cm by 14 cm. Metallic ribbon, 2 cm by 50 cm.

FINISHED SIZE: 14 cm by 78.5 cm.

DIRECTIONS: Trace actual size pattern. Transfer design to fabric, starting from bottom. Reverse arrangement for upper half. Work all embroidery in long and short stitch with two strands of floss in needle unless otherwise indicated. When embroidery is finished, place iron-on interfacing on wrong side of embroidered piece and press. Turn raw edges of both sides 2 cm each to wrong side. Place lining 1 cm inside from folded edges. Slip stitch. Turn 0.5 cm raw edges at top to wrong side and then turn down 1.5 cm. Slip stitch top hem in place. Hem in same manner at bottom. Insert hanger into top hem and weight into bottom hem. Tie ribbon into bow and sew in place.

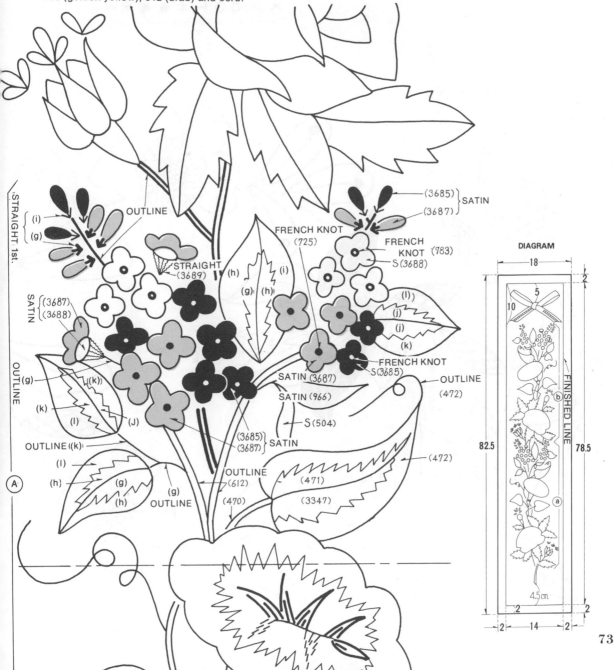

73

MATERIALS

Fabric: Beige silk, 21.5 cm by 94 cm.

Beige cotton satin for lining, 19 cm by 92 cm.

Threads: D.M.C. # 25 six-strand embroidery floss.

1 skein each of 351 (geranium red), 760 (morocco red), 732 (yellow green) and 816 (scarlet). ½ skein each of 349, 350, 352 (geranium red), 304, 815 (scarlet), 321 (turkey red), 947 (fire red), 347 (cardinal red), 831, 832 (copper green), 733 and 734 (yellow green). Small amount each of 725 (saffron), 729 (old gold), 977 (umber gold), 783 (cornflower blue) and 902 (scarlet).

One set of bell pull attachments. Iron-on interfacing, 90 cm by 17.5 cm.

FINISHED SIZE: See diagram.

DIRECTIONS: Trace actual size pattern. Transfer design to fabric (see diagram). Work all embroidery with two strands of floss in needle unless otherwise indicated. When embroidery is finished, place iron-on interfacing on wrong side of embroidered piece and press. Make side hems, and top and bottom hems in same manner as indicated on page 73. Insert hanger into top hem and weight into bottom hem.

= 732	= 733	= 832	= 831	= 816	= 902	= 580	= 581	= 936
×	∨	◀	○	T	‡	●	◀	✳

SATIN STITCH

LINING

19

SEAM ALLOWANCE

90

92

17

1

1

FINISHED DIAGRAM

2cm

HANGER

90 cm

17.5 cm

2cm

WEIGHT

19 cm

91.5 cm

DIAGRAM

2

90

2

21.5

25.5 cm

A

A

B

B

A

25.5 cm

A

B

17.5

CENTER

FINISHED LINE

2

2

2

94

CENTER

(936)

FRENCH KNOT FILLING 3st.
(725)

(349)
(351) } LONG & SHORT

OUTLINE (832)

SATIN

(581)

CENTER

(581)

SATIN(581)

SATIN(349)

(350)
(352) } LONG & SHORT

*

(732)

X

X

FLOWER Ⓑ

(347)
(760) } LONG & SHORT

FRENCH KNOT FILLING
(977) 3st.

(581)

FRENCH KNOT
FILLING(729)3st.

(350)
(352) } LONG & SHORT

B

CENTER

X

V

(732)

(815)
(321) } SATIN

T

T

╬

T

SATIN (304)

CLOSED HERRINGBONE (732)

75

MATERIALS

Fabric: Grey silk satin, 50 cm by 46 cm.
Grey velveteen, 90 cm by 80 cm.
Threads: D.M.C. #25 six-strand embroidery floss.
4 skeins each of 926 (myrtle grey) and 519 (sky blue).
3 skeins each of 927 (myrtle grey) and 518 (sky blue).
1 skein each of 963 (magenta rose), 3350 and 3354 (old rose).
One zipper, 38 cm long. Inner pillow stuffed with 500 grams of kapok. Cord, 0.6 cm in diameter and 220 cm long.

FINISHED SIZE: See diagram.

DIRECTIONS: Trace pattern. Transfer design to fabric reversing arrangement for right side. Work embroidery as indicated. Cut velveteen (see cutting layout). Sew zipper to back piece. Join three strips of velveteen to make a circle. Turn to right side and fold in half lengthwise. Insert cord and pull ends of cord until they meet. Distribute gathers evenly. Place ruffle against right side of front (embroidered) piece with raw edges together. Make pleats evenly to fit. With right sides of front and back facing, and ruffle between, stitch around four sides. Turn right side out, and insert inner pillow.

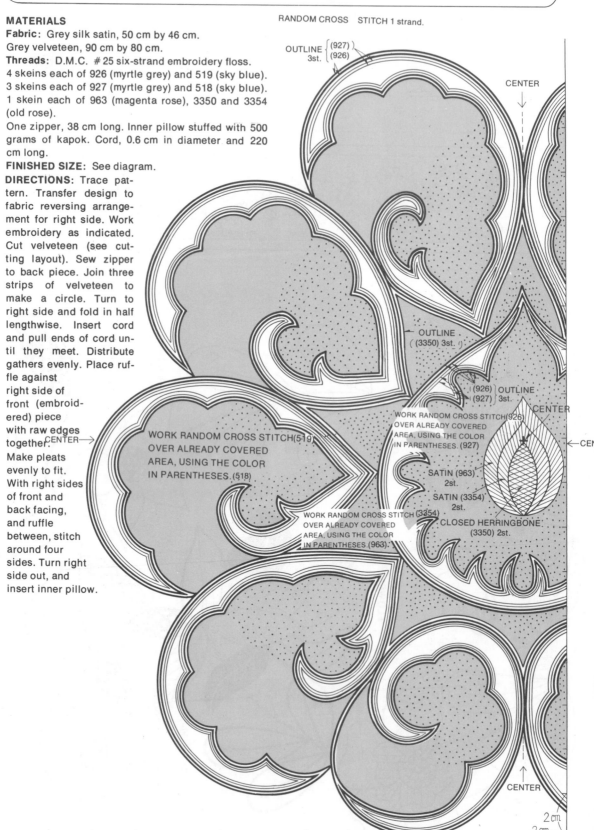

RANDOM CROSS   STITCH 1 strand.

OUTLINE 3st. { (927) (926) }

CENTER

OUTLINE ((3350) 3st.)

((926) (927)) OUTLINE 3st.

CENTER

WORK RANDOM CROSS STITCH(926) OVER ALREADY COVERED AREA, USING THE COLOR IN PARENTHESES. (927)

WORK RANDOM CROSS STITCH(519) OVER ALREADY COVERED AREA, USING THE COLOR IN PARENTHESES. (518)

CENT

SATIN (963) 2st.

SATIN (3354) 2st.

WORK RANDOM CROSS STITCH (3354) OVER ALREADY COVERED AREA, USING THE COLOR IN PARENTHESES (963).

CLOSED HERRINGBONE (3350) 2st.

CENTER

CENTER

2 cm
2 cm

76

CUTTING LAYOUT (VELVETEEN)

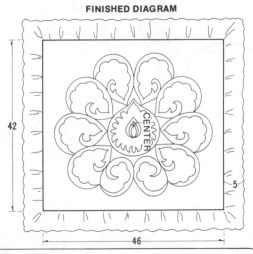

```
12  ↕   FRILL
12  ↕   FRILL
12  ↕   FRILL

80
44    FINISHED LINE   BACK   ZIPPER   5  5   ZIPPER   BACK   42
      1                2  38=        5 5   2  38=        2
                      30         2       2  16          1
      1 SEAM ALLOWANCE    58              90
```

FINISHED DIAGRAM

```
42                      CENTER
                                        5
        46
```

FLORAL BEDSPREAD   shown on page 15

MATERIALS

Fabric: Ivory silk for embroidery, 70 cm by 243.5 cm.
Beige lawn for lining, 70 cm by 243.5 cm.
Heavy-weight moss green silk for both sides and border, 90 cm by 710 cm.

Threads: D.M.C. #25 six-strand embroidery floss.
8 skeins of 3053 (green). 7 skeins of 741 (tangerine yellow). 4 skeins each of 319, 367 (pistachio green), 742 (tangerine yellow), 758 (terra-cotta) and 3042 (Indian red). 3 skeins each of 356 (terra-cotta), 921 (red brown), 3041 (Indian red), 3051 (green) and 3687 (raspberry red). 2 skeins each of 355 (terra-cotta), 731, 733 (yellow green), 743 (tangerine yellow), 783 (golden yellow) and 3685 (raspberry red). 1 skein each of 453 (seagull grey), 613 (drab), 827 (forget-me-not blue), 932 (antique blue), 950 (chestnut), 976 (umber gold), 3012 and 3013 (sage green). Small amount each of 502 and 503 (almond green).

Braid, 6.5 cm by 487 cm.

FINISHED SIZE: 257.5 cm by 221 cm.

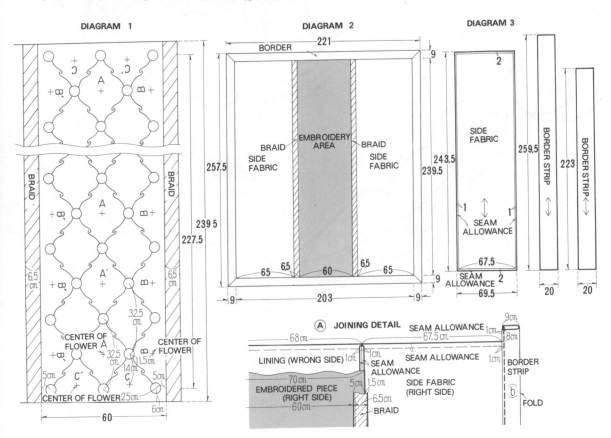

DIAGRAM 1

DIAGRAM 2

DIAGRAM 3

A JOINING DETAIL

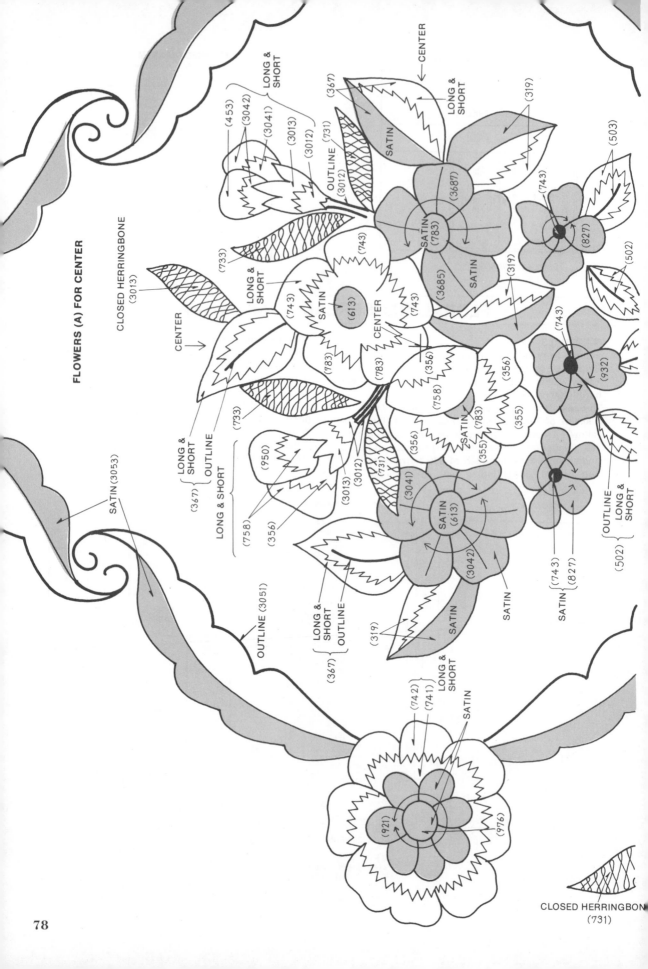

FLOWERS (A) FOR CENTER

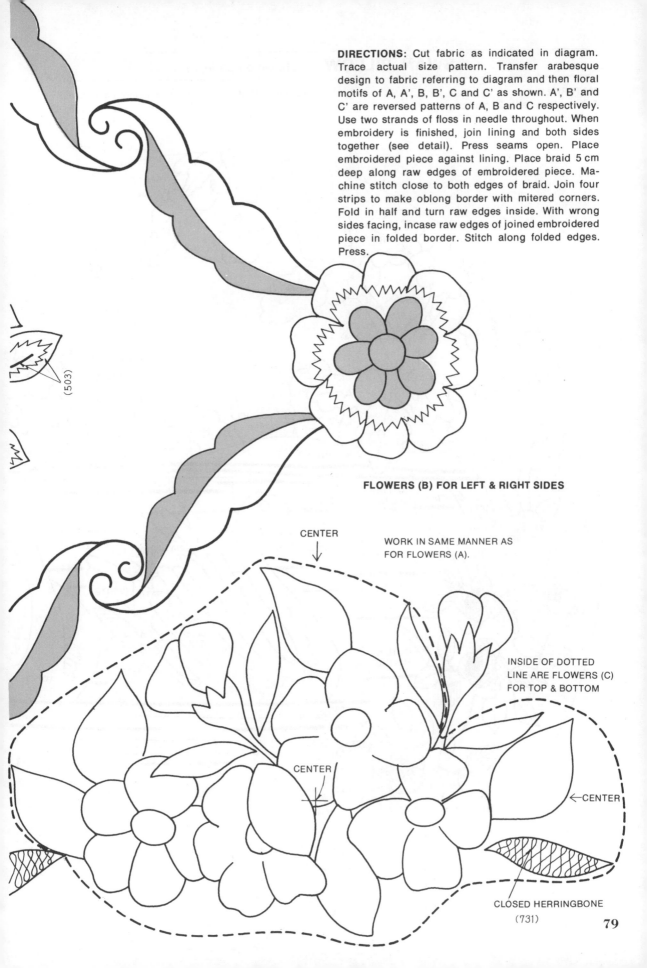

DIRECTIONS: Cut fabric as indicated in diagram. Trace actual size pattern. Transfer arabesque design to fabric referring to diagram and then floral motifs of A, A', B, B', C and C' as shown. A', B' and C' are reversed patterns of A, B and C respectively. Use two strands of floss in needle throughout. When embroidery is finished, join lining and both sides together (see detail). Press seams open. Place embroidered piece against lining. Place braid 5 cm deep along raw edges of embroidered piece. Machine stitch close to both edges of braid. Join four strips to make oblong border with mitered corners. Fold in half and turn raw edges inside. With wrong sides facing, incase raw edges of joined embroidered piece in folded border. Stitch along folded edges. Press.

(503)

FLOWERS (B) FOR LEFT & RIGHT SIDES

CENTER

WORK IN SAME MANNER AS FOR FLOWERS (A).

INSIDE OF DOTTED LINE ARE FLOWERS (C) FOR TOP & BOTTOM

CENTER

CENTER

CLOSED HERRINGBONE
(731)

79

MATERIALS

Fabric: Beige silk, 25 cm square.
Blue velveteen, 57 cm by 150 cm.

Threads: D.M.C. #25 six-strand embroidery floss.
1 sekin of white. ½ skein each of 986, 987, 988, 989
(laurel green), 580 (golden green), 469, 470, 471,

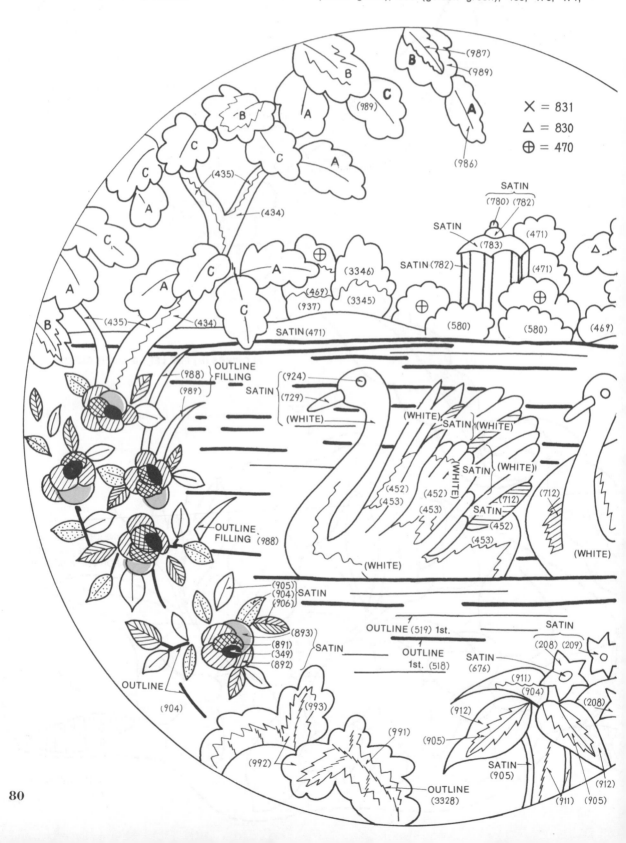

80

472 (moss green), 830, 831 (copper green), 434, 435 (umber), 904, 905, 906 (parakeet green), 891, 892, 893 (geranium pink), 349 (geranium red), 992 (peacock green), 911, 912 (emerald green), 518 and 519 (sky blue). Small amount each of 937 (moss green), 3345, 3346 (scarab green), 832 (copper green), 436 (umber), 780, 782, 783 (golden yellow), 3328 (morocco red), 993, 991 (peacock green), 208, 209 (parma violet), 676 (old gold), 452, 453 (seagull grey), 712 (corn yellow), 924 (myrtle grey) and 729 (old gold). Golden braid, 1 cm by 70 cm. Inner pillow stuffed with 450 grams of kapok.

FINISHED SIZE: 43 cm in diameter.
DIRECTIONS: Trace actual size pattern. Transfer design to beige silk. Work all embroidery in long and short stitch with two strands of floss in needle unless otherwise indicated. When embroidery is finished, press. Cut out circle of 23 cm in diameter (including 1 cm seam allowance around). Cut two pieces of gusset and one back. Join two pieces of gusset to make circle. Machine stitch along both edges to gather. Distribute gathers evenly. With right sides of embroidered piece and gusset together, sew around edges. Insert inner pillow. Place back piece against gusset turn raw edge under and slip stitch. Slip stitch braid along seam line of front.

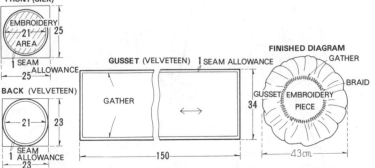

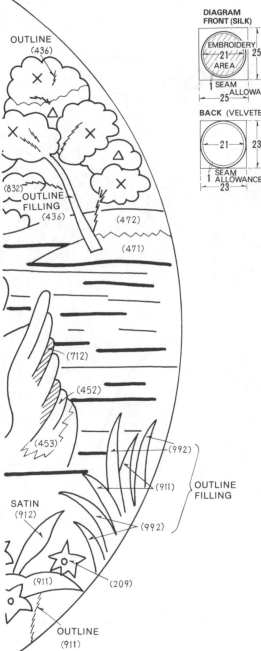

FAIRY TALE PILLOW
shown on page 17

MATERIALS
Fabric: Pink silk, 92 cm by 84 cm.
Threads: D.M.C. #25 six-strand embroidery floss.
2 skeins of 3325 (azure blue). 1 skein of 603 (cerise). ½ skein each of white, 893 (geranium pink), 676 (old gold), 899, 3326 (soft pink), 3051 (green), 367, 320 (pistachio green), 988, 989 (laurel green), 225 (faded pink), 783 (golden yellow), 327 (violet mauve), 712 (corn yellow) and écru. Small amount each of 892, 894 (geranium pink), 677 (old gold), 309, 335 (garnet red), 961, 962, 963 (magenta rose), 600, 602 (cerise), 818 (soft pink), 224 (faded pink), 799 (Sèvres blue), 992, 993 (peacock green), 210 (parma violet), 744 (tangerine yellow), 317, 318, 415 (ash grey), 453 (seagull grey), 729 (old gold), 304 (Indian red), 554 (plum), 3052 (green), 368 (pistachio green), 937, 469 (moss green), 806 (peacock blue), 517 and 518 (sky blue).
One zipper, 40 cm long. Inner pilow stuffed with 450 grams of kapok.
FINISHED SIZE: See diagram.
DIRECTIONS: Cut fabric referring to cutting diagram. Trace actual size pattern. Transfer design to fabric reversing arrangement for ribbons at corners. Work all embroidery in long and short stitch with two strands of floss in needle unless otherwise indicated. Join four strips to make a circle. Turn right side out. Fold in half lengthwise and machine stitch along seam line to gather. Baste ruffle to right side of embroidered piece distributing gathers evenly. With right sides of embroidered and back pieces facing, and ruffle between, stitch around all edges. Press. Turn right side out and insert inner pillow.

L=LONG & SHORT STITCH
S=SATIN STITCH

S (988)

A

S(WHITE)
STRAIGHT(893)

B

B

C

S (893)
S (676)
STRAIGHT(892)

A

CHAIN(603)
S(783)

OUTLINE
(783)

S(989)

OUTLINE
(988)

C

S (3326)

(899)
S (309)
(335)

(961)
(962) STRAIGHT

S (367)

CHAIN
(602)

OUTLINE
(806)

S
(320)

(992)
(806) S
(224)

S
(989)

A

S

(517)
(518)

L
(937)

L
(3051)

L (368)

S(806)   S(415)

S(317)

L (320)
(367)

B

B

A

BULLION
ROSE
(600,603)
IN OUT

L (677)

STRAIGHT
(799)

S
(225)

STRAIGHT
(799)
(899)
(602)

L
(603)

FRENCH
KNOT
(712)

BULLION
KNOT (ÉCRU)

OUTLINE (318)
OUTLINE
FILLING (ÉCRU)

(327)
(WHITE) S
(676)

L
(327)

S
(225)

S
(3041)

L
(712)

L
(327)

L
(603)

OUTLINE
(963)
1 st.

S (327)
(712)

ROUMANIAN
COUCHING
(453)

C

82

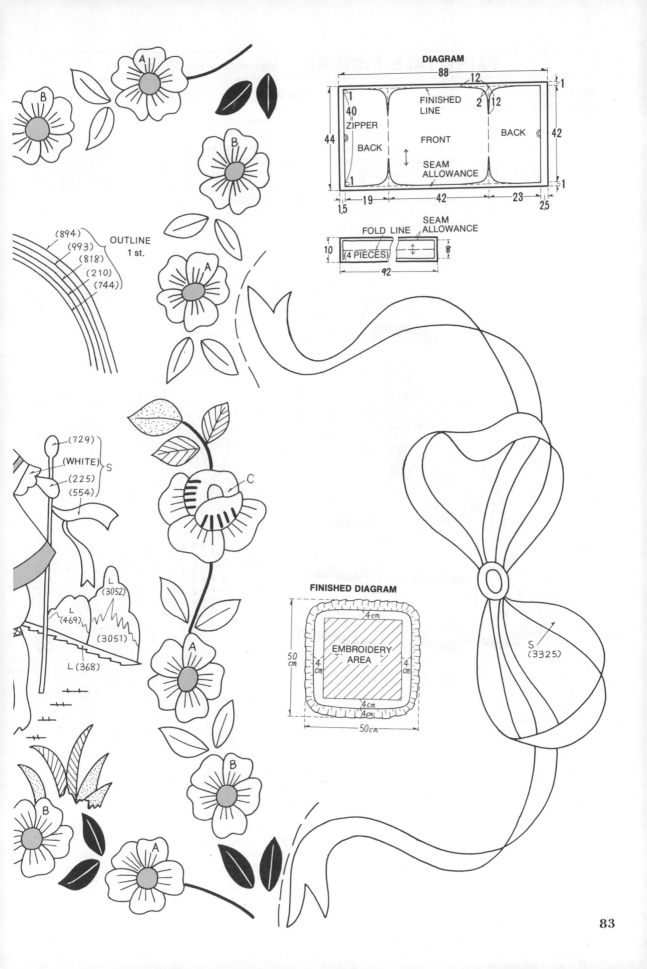

DIAGRAM

88

12

1

1

40

ZIPPER

FINISHED
LINE

2

12

44

BACK

FRONT

BACK

42

1

SEAM
ALLOWANCE

1

1.5

19

42

23

2.5

FOLD LINE

SEAM
ALLOWANCE

10

(4 PIECES)

8

92

OUTLINE
1 st.

(894)
(993)
(818)
(210)
(744)

(729)
(WHITE)
(225)
(554)

S

C

L
(3052)

L
(469)

L
(3051)

L (368)

A

B

FINISHED DIAGRAM

4 cm

50
cm

EMBROIDERY
AREA

4
cm

4
cm

4 cm

4 cm

50 cm

S
(3325)

MATERIALS

Fabric: White linen, 25 cm square.

Threads: D.M.C. #25 six-strand embroidery floss. 1 sekin each of 603, 604 (cerise) and 327 (violet mauve). ½ skein each of 928 (myrtle grey), 602 (cerise) and 704 (brilliant green). Small amount each of 729 (old gold), 644 (smoke grey), 3041, 3042 (Indian red), 452 (seagull grey), 225 (faded pink), 926 (myrtle grey), 911 (emerald green), 892, 893 (geranium pink), 350 (geranium red), 601, 605 (cerise), 727 (saffron), 819 (soft pink), 992 (peacock green), 799 (Sèvres blue) and white.

Frame, 19.5 cm square (inside measurement).

FINISHED SIZE: Same size as frame.

DIRECTIONS: Trace actual size pattern. Transfer design to fabric. Work all embroidery in satin stitch with two strands of floss in needle unless otherwise indicated. Press, when embroidery is finished. Mount and frame.

WAVE STITCH

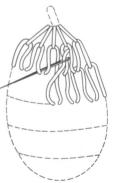

MATERIALS

Fabric: White linen, 25 cm square.

Threads: D.M.C. #25 six-strand embroidery floss. 1 sekin each of 806 (peacock blue), 326 (garnet red) and 893 (geranium pink). ½ skein each of 725 (saffron), 415 (ash grey), 712 (corn yellow), 676 (old gold), 553 (plum) and 894 (geranium pink). Small amount each of 644 (smoke grey), 727 (saffron), 317 (ash grey), 783 (golden yellow), 225 (faded pink), 799 (Sèvres blue), 718 (episcopal purple), 552, 554 (plum), 892 (geranium pink), 210 (parma violet), 819 (soft pink), 911 (emerald green), 350 (geranium red) and white.

Frame, 19.5 cm square (inside measurement).

FINISHED SIZE: Same size as frame.

DIRECTIONS: Trace actual size pattern. Transfer design to fabric. Work all embroidery in satin stitch with two strands of floss in needle unless otherwise indicated. Press, when embroidery is finished. Mount and frame.

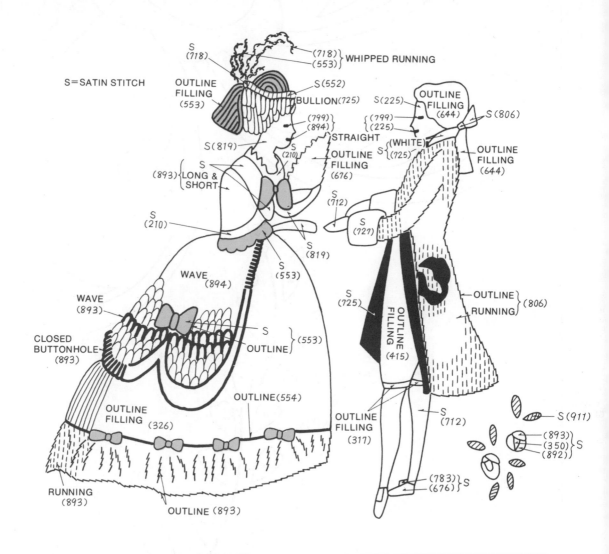

S=SATIN STITCH

(718) (553) } WHIPPED RUNNING

S (718)

OUTLINE FILLING (553)

S(552)

BULLION(725)

(799) (894)

S(819)

S (210)

STRAIGHT

OUTLINE FILLING (676)

(893) } LONG & SHORT

S

S (210)

(712)

S (819)

S (553)

WAVE (894)

WAVE (893)

CLOSED BUTTONHOLE (893)

S } (553)

OUTLINE

OUTLINE FILLING (326)

OUTLINE(554)

RUNNING (893)

OUTLINE (893)

S(225)

OUTLINE FILLING (644)

S(806)

(799) (225)

(WHITE) (725)

S

OUTLINE FILLING (644)

S (727)

S (725)

OUTLINE FILLING (415)

OUTLINE RUNNING } (806)

OUTLINE FILLING (317)

S (712)

S (712)

S (911)

(893) (350) (892) } S

(783) (676) } S

TABLECLOTH shown on pages 18–19

MATERIALS

Fabric: White cotton organdy, 90 cm square.

Threads: D.M.C. # 25 six-strand embroidery floss.

4 skeins of white. 1 skein each of 320, 368 (pistachio green), 307, 445 (lemon yellow), 444 (buttercup yellow), 471, 472 (moss green), 744 (tangerine yellow), 907 (parakeet green), 899 (soft pink) and 963 (magenta rose). ½ skein each of 209, 211 (parma violet), 502 (almond green), 519 (sky blue), 809 and 813 (forget-me-not blue). Small amount each of 503 (almond green), 776 (soft pink), 894 (geranium pink), 3013 (sage green), 3047 (beige) and 3348 (scarab green).

White lace, 1.5 cm by 360 cm.

FINISHED SIZE: 88.5 cm square.

DIRECTIONS: Trace actual size pattern. Transfer design to fabric reversing arrangement for the other half and the remaining three quarters. (see diagram). Work all embroidery in shadow stitch with two strands of floss in needle unless otherwise indicated. Cut out 87 cm square. Make narrow hem. Place white lace 0.3 cm deep along folded edges. Slip stitch.

FINISHED DIAGRAM

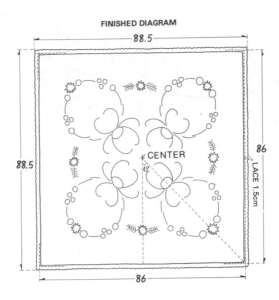

88.5

88.5

CENTER

86

LACE 1.5cm

86

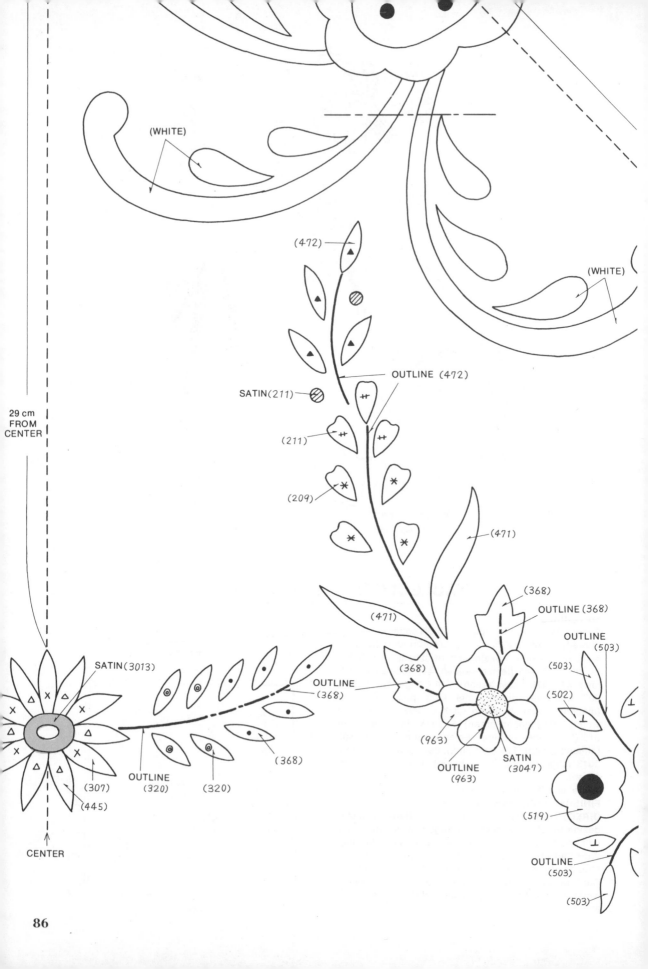

WHITE

WHITE

SATIN
(WHITE)

40.5 cm
FROM
CENTER

(320)

(894)   (776)

OUTLINE
(320)

(813)

SATIN
(WHITE)

OUTLINE(907)

SATIN
(368)

OUTLINE
(368)

(907)

(776)

(320)

(307)

(444)

SATIN
(3013)

OUTLINE
(3348)

(899)

SATIN (744)

OUTLINE(899)

(809)

OUTLINE
(320)

(907)

OUTLINE(907)

87

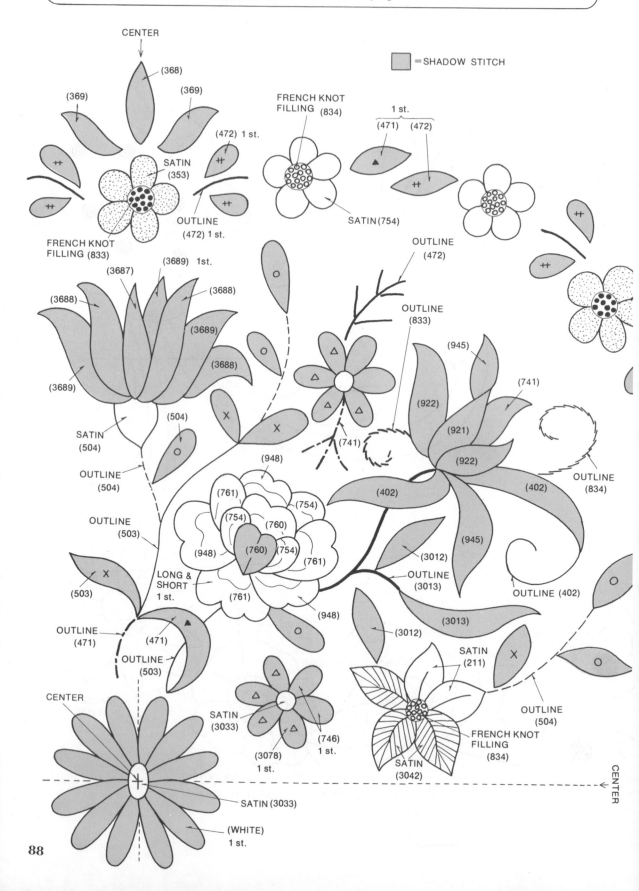

PILLOW shown on page 20

= SHADOW STITCH

CENTER
(368)
(369)
(369)
SATIN (353)
(472) 1 st.
FRENCH KNOT FILLING (834)
1 st. (471) (472)
OUTLINE (472) 1 st.
FRENCH KNOT FILLING (833)
SATIN (754)
OUTLINE (472)
(3689) 1st.
(3687)
(3688)
(3688)
(3689)
(3688)
(3689)
OUTLINE (833)
(945)
(741)
(922)
(921)
(922)
OUTLINE (834)
SATIN (504)
(504)
(402)
(402)
OUTLINE (504)
(948)
(741)
OUTLINE (503)
(761)
(754)
(754)
(760)
(948)
(760)
(754)
(761)
(945)
(503)
(948)
LONG & SHORT 1 st.
(761)
(3012)
OUTLINE (3013)
OUTLINE (402)
OUTLINE (471)
(471)
OUTLINE (503)
(948)
(3013)
SATIN (211)
CENTER
SATIN (3033)
(3078) 1 st.
(746) 1 st.
(3012)
OUTLINE (504)
FRENCH KNOT FILLING (834)
SATIN (3042)
CENTER
SATIN (3033)
(WHITE) 1 st.

88

MATERIALS

Fabric: White cotton organdy, 90 cm by 100 cm. Light-weight white linen for lining, 90 cm by 100 cm.

Threads: D.M.C. #25 six-strand embroidery floss. 1½ skeins of 754 (geranium red). 1 skein each of 353 (geranium red), 3042 (Indian red) and 211 (parma violet). ½ skein each of 760, 761 (morocco red), 948 (geranium red), 503, 504 (almond green), 471, 472 (moss green), 368 (pistachio green), 3012, 3013 (sage green), 833, 834 (copper green), 3033 (dark brown), 921, 922 (red brown), 402 (mahogany), 741, 742 (tangerine yellow), 3687, 3688 and 3689 (raspberry red). Small amount each of 3078 (light yellow), 746 (cream) and white.

One zipper, 40 cm long. Inner pillow stuffed with 400 grms. of kapok. 4-ply yarn in white, 6m.

FINISHED SIZE: See diagram.

DIRECTIONS: Cut outer fabric and lining referring to cutting layout. Trace actual size pattern. Transfer design to fabric reversing design for left side and bottom half (see diagram). Use two strands of floss in needle unless otherwise indicated. When embroidery is finished, press. Place wrong side of embroidered piece against right side of white linen for front. Baste together along all edges. Line back piece and four strips for ruffle with linen in same manner. Sew zipper to lined back piece. Join four lined strips together to make a circle. Fold in half lengthwise. With right sides together, stitch along all edges with 1 cm seam allowance leaving 10 cm opening. Turn to right side. Insert three 2m length of yarn into ruffle and pull ends of yarns. Tie ends of yarns together. Slip stitch opening closed. Distribute gathers evenly. With right sides together, stitch along all edges with 3.5 cm seam allowance. Turn inside out. Slip stitch ruffle along four edges.

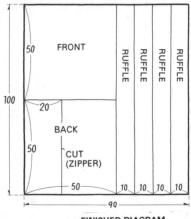

CUTTING LAYOUT FOR OUTER FABRIC & LINING

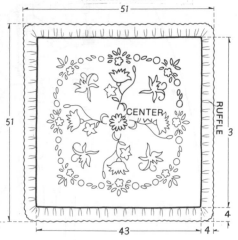

FINISHED DIAGRAM

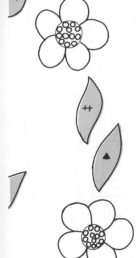

OVAL FRAMED PICTURE

shown on page 17, bottom

MATERIALS

Fabric: Off-white linen, 30 cm by 25 cm.

Threads: D.M.C. #25 six-strand embroidery floss. 1 skein of 437 (umber). ½ skein each of 517, 519, 747 (sky blue), 920 (red brown), 676, 729 (old gold), 930 (antique blue), 3328 (morocco red), 318 (ash grey), 613 (drab), 422 (hazel-nut brown), 738 (umber), 319, 320, 367, 368, 369 (pistachio green), 469, 937 (moss green), 3346 and 3347 (scarab green). Small amount each of 839 (beige brown), 351 (geranium red), 356 (terra-cotta), 760, 761 (morocco red), 223, 224 (faded pink), 316 (dull mauve), 924, 926 (myrtle grey), 414 (ash grey), 950 (chestnut), 948 (geranium red), 433 (umber), 347 (cardinal red) and white.

Oval frame, 19 cm by 14 cm (inside measurement).

FINISHED SIZE: 20.5 cm by 15.5 cm oval.

DIRECTIONS: Trace actual size pattern. Transfer design to fabric. Work all embroidery in satin stitch with two strands of floss in needle unless otherwise indicated. Press, when embroidery is finished. Mount and frame.

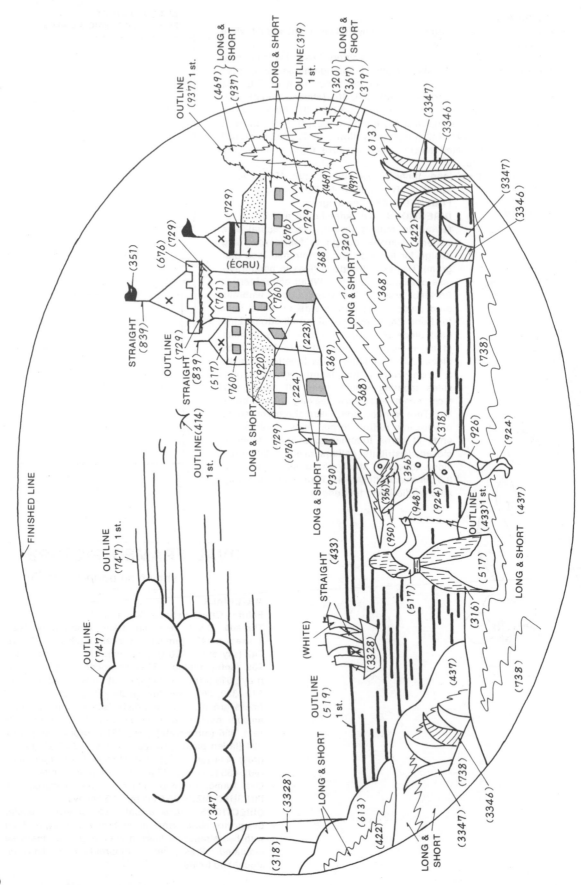

TABLECLOTH   shown on page 22

MATERIALS

Fabric: Light-weight white line, 91 cm by 133 cm for embroidery and 52 cm by 145 cm for border.

Threads: D.M.C. #25 six-strand embroidery floss. 7 skeins of white. 1 skein each of 818, 899, 3326 (soft pink), 744 (tangerine yellow), 726, 727 (saffron), 783 (dull mauve), 798, 799, 800 (Sèvres blue), 809 (forget-me-not blue), 502 and 503 (almond green). Small amount each of 209, 211 (parma violet), 553 (plum), 335 (garnet red), 3688 and 3689 (raspberry red).

FINISHED SIZE: 144 cm by 102 cm.

DIRECTIONS: Trace actual size pattern. Transfer design to fabric referring to diagram. Use two strands of floss for shadow stitch and one strand of floss for satin and outline stitches throughout. Join four strips to make oblong border with mitered corners. Fold in half and turn raw edges inside. With wrong sides facing, incase raw edges of embroidered piece in folded border, overlapping 0.5 cm seam allowances. Stitch along folded edges. Press.

DIAGRAM

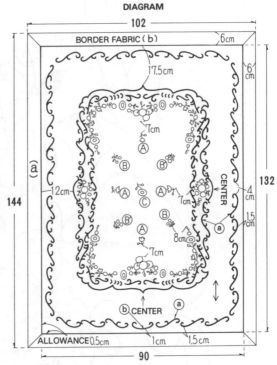

DIAGRAM FOR BORDER FABRIC

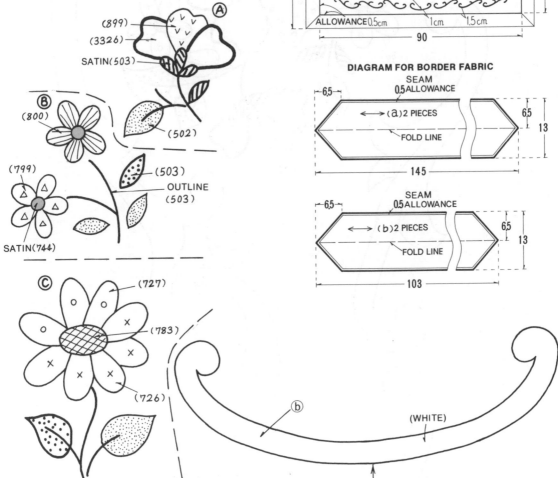

91

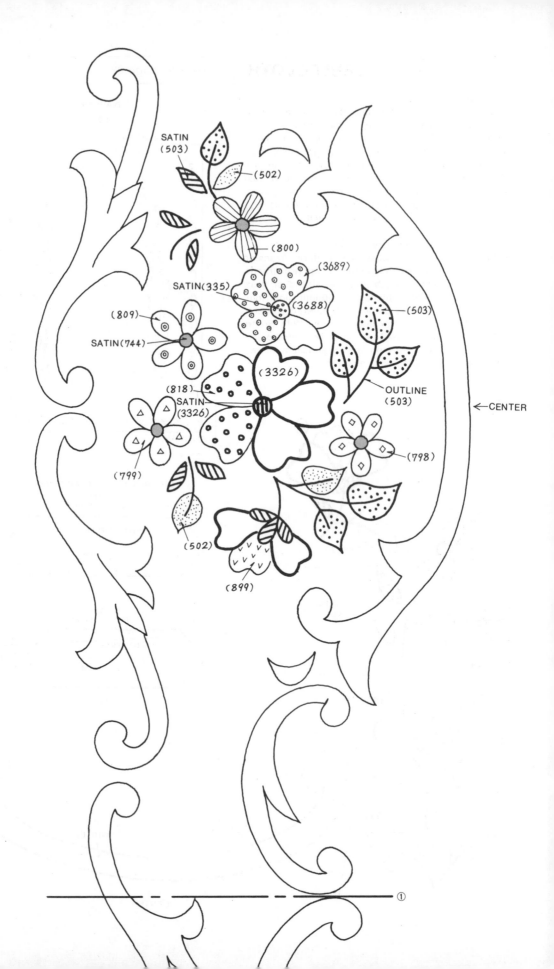

SATIN (503)
(502)
(800)
(3689)
SATIN(335)
(809)
(3688)
SATIN(744)
(503)
(3326)
(818)
OUTLINE (503)
SATIN (3326)
←CENTER
(799)
(798)
(502)
(899)

①

SATIN
(503)

(726)

(783)

(727)

(502)

OUTLINE
(503)

(809)

(798)

SATIN(502)

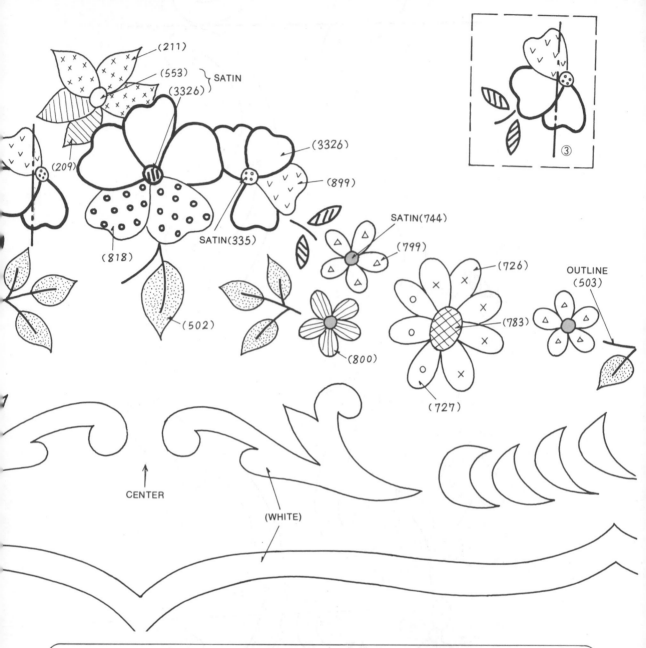

(211)

(553) } SATIN

(3326)

(3326)

(209)

(899)

SATIN(744)

(799)

(726)

OUTLINE
(503)

SATIN(335)

(818)

(502)

(800)

(783)

(727)

CENTER

(WHITE)

LAMPSHADE AND MATCHING TABLE CENTER shown on page 21

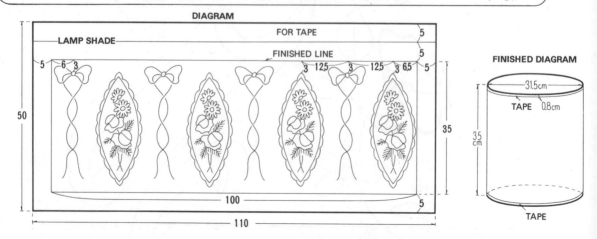

DIAGRAM

FOR TAPE

LAMP SHADE

FINISHED LINE

5   6 3

3 12.5   3   12.5   3 6.5   5

50

35

100

5

110

FINISHED DIAGRAM

31.5cm

TAPE   0.8cm

35
cm

TAPE

(502)
(503) } SATIN

MATERIALS

Fabric: Swiss-made white cotton organdy, 110 cm by 50 cm for lampshade. Swiss-made cotton organdy, 70 cm by 40 cm for table center.

FINISHED DIAGRAM

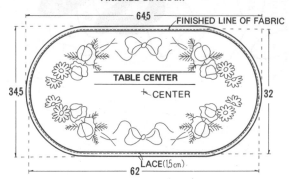

FINISHED LINE OF FABRIC

64,5

TABLE CENTER

CENTER

34,5

32

LACE(1.5 cm)

62

Threads: D.M.C. #25 six-strand embroidery floss.
FOR LAMPSHADE
2 skeins each of 320 (pistachio green), 3688 and 3689 (raspberry red) and white. 1 skein each of 335 (garnet red), 962, 963 (magenta rose), 899, 3326 (soft pink), 3687 (raspberry red), 368 (pistachio green), 799 (Sèvres blue) and 809 (forget-me-not blue). Small amount each of 745 (tangerine yellow), 758 (terra-cotta), 3347 and 3348 (scarab green).
FOR TABLE CENTER
2 skeins each of 320 (pistachio green) and 3688 (raspberry red). 1 skein each of 335 (garnet red), 962, 963 (magenta rose), 899, 3326 (soft pink), 3687, 3689 (raspberry red), 519 (sky blue), 799 (Sèvres blue), 809 (forget-me-not blue) and 368 (pistachio green). Small amount each of 745 (tangerine yellow), 758 (terra-cotta), 3347 and 3348 (scarab green). White lace for table center, 1.5 cm by 140 cm.

95

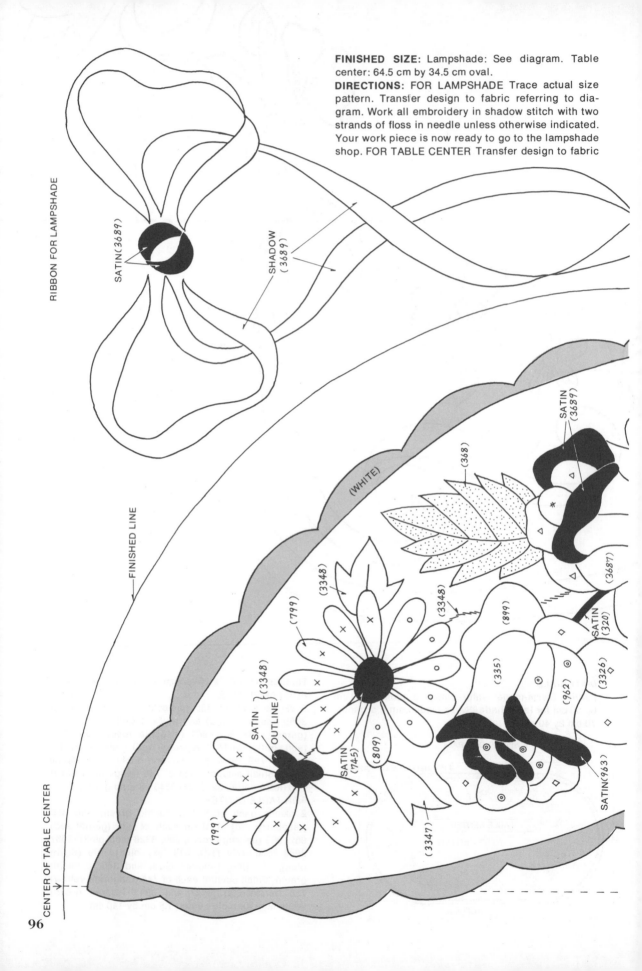

RIBBON FOR LAMPSHADE

SATIN(3689)

SHADOW
(3689)

FINISHED SIZE: Lampshade: See diagram. Table center: 64.5 cm by 34.5 cm oval.
DIRECTIONS: FOR LAMPSHADE Trace actual size pattern. Transfer design to fabric referring to diagram. Work all embroidery in shadow stitch with two strands of floss in needle unless otherwise indicated. Your work piece is now ready to go to the lampshade shop. FOR TABLE CENTER Transfer design to fabric

SATIN
(3689)

(368)

(WHITE)

(3687)

(3348)

(3348)

SATIN
(320)

FINISHED LINE

(799)

(899)

(335)

(962)

(3326)

SATIN
OUTLINE } (3348)

SATIN
(745)

(809)

SATIN(963)

(3347)

CENTER OF TABLE CENTER

(799)

(3347)

referring to diagram. Work in same manner as for lampshade. When embroidery is finished, machine stitch along fold line. Cut out 0.3 cm outside from stitching. Turn 0.3 cm to right side along stitching. Slip stitch white lace 0.3 cm deep along hem.

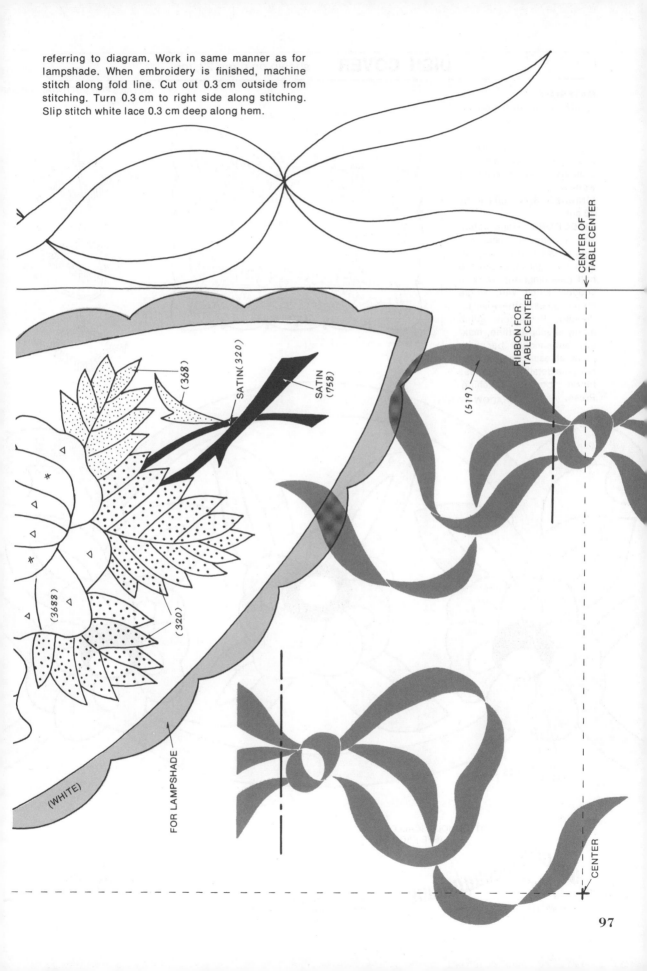

CENTER OF
TABLE CENTER

RIBBON FOR
TABLE CENTER

(519)

(368)

SATIN(320)

SATIN
(758)

(320)

(3688)

(WHITE)

FOR LAMPSHADE

CENTER

DISH COVER   shown on page 23, top

MATERIALS

Fabric: White cotton organdy, 55 cm by 45 cm.

Threads: D.M.C. à broder #20, 3 skeins of white. D.M.C. #25 six-strand embroidery floss, 1 skein of white.

FINISHED SIZE: 50 cm by 39 cm.

DIRECTIONS: Trace actual size pattern. Transfer design to fabric, reversing design for right side and top half (see diagram). Work in shadow stitch with single strand unless otherwise indicated. Buttonhole stitch along scallop outline, making buttonholed bar with picot at each wedged corner (see detail). Trim excess fabric beyond stitching. Press.

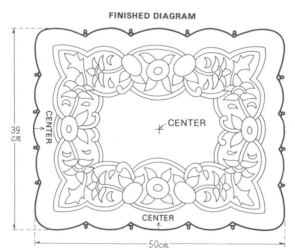

FINISHED DIAGRAM

CENTER

CENTER

CENTER

39 cm

50 cm

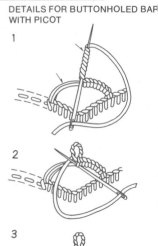

DETAILS FOR BUTTONHOLED BAR WITH PICOT

1

2

3

SHADOW STITCH

BACK
SATIN } #25, 2 st.

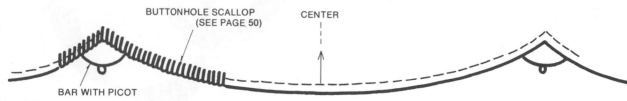

BUTTONHOLE SCALLOP
(SEE PAGE 50)

CENTER

BAR WITH PICOT

CENTER

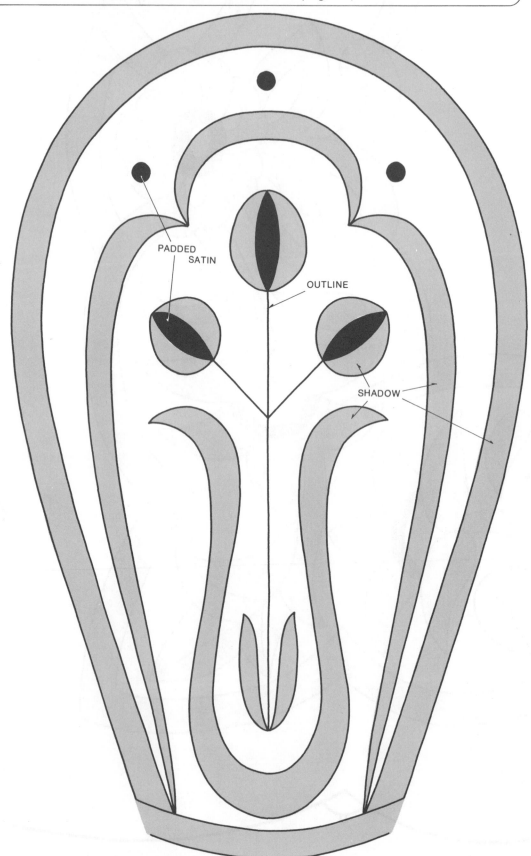

PADDED SATIN

OUTLINE

SHADOW

MATERIALS

Fabric: White cotton organdy, 80 cm square.
Threads: D.M.C. à broder #25, 4 skeins of white. White lace, 1.5 cm by 245 cm.
FINISHED SIZE: 77.5 cm in diameter.
DIRECTIONS: Trace actual size pattern. Transfer design to center of fabric (see diagram). Work in shadow stitch with single strand unless otherwise indicated. When embroidery is finished, machine stitch around 75 cm-diameter circle. Cut out circle 0.3 cm outside from stitching. Turn raw edge along stitching to right side. Place white lace 0.2 cm deep along folded edge and slip stitch. Press.

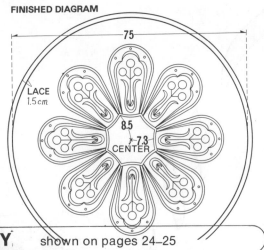

TABLECLOTH AND DOILY shown on pages 24–25

MATERIALS

Fabric: White linen, 130cm by 186 cm for tablecloth. White linen, 77 cm by 51cm for doily.
Threads: D.M.C. #25 six-strand embroidery floss.
FOR TABLE CLOTH
12 skeins of 3042 (Indian red). 6 skeins of 327 (violet mauve). 5 skeins of 3354 (old rose). 4 skeins of 367 (pistachio green), 3 skeins of 309 (garnet red). 2 skeins each of 471 (moss green), 335 (garnet red) and 320 (pistachio green). 1 skein each of 727 (saf-fron) and 972 (canary yellow). ½ skein of 726 (saffron).

FOR DOILY
2 skeins of 3042 (Indian red). 1 skein each of 327 (violet mauve) and 3354 (old rose). Small amount each of 320, 367 (pistachio green), 726, 727 (saffron), 972 (canary yellow), 309 and 335 (garnet red).

FINISHED SIZE: Tablecloth, 174 cm by 118 cm. Doily, 69 cm by 43 cm.

DIRECTIONS: FOR TABLECLOTH Trace actual size pattern. Transfer design to fabric (see diagram). Work all embroidery in satin stitch with two strands of floss in needle unless otherwise indicated. Outline stitch with three strands of floss along hemline. Finish edges with 3 cm deep hem, mitering corners neatly. Press. FOR DOILY Transfer design to fabric (see diagram). Work in same manner as for tablecloth but use two strands of floss in needle for outline stitch along hemline. Finish edges with 2 cm hem, mitering corners neatly. Press.

DIAGRAM OF TABLECLOTH

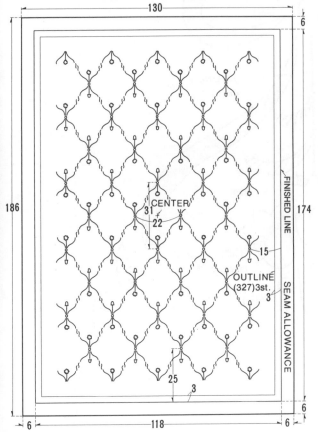

DIAGRAM OF DOILY

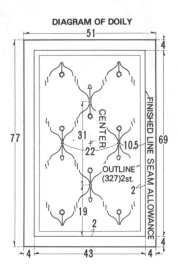

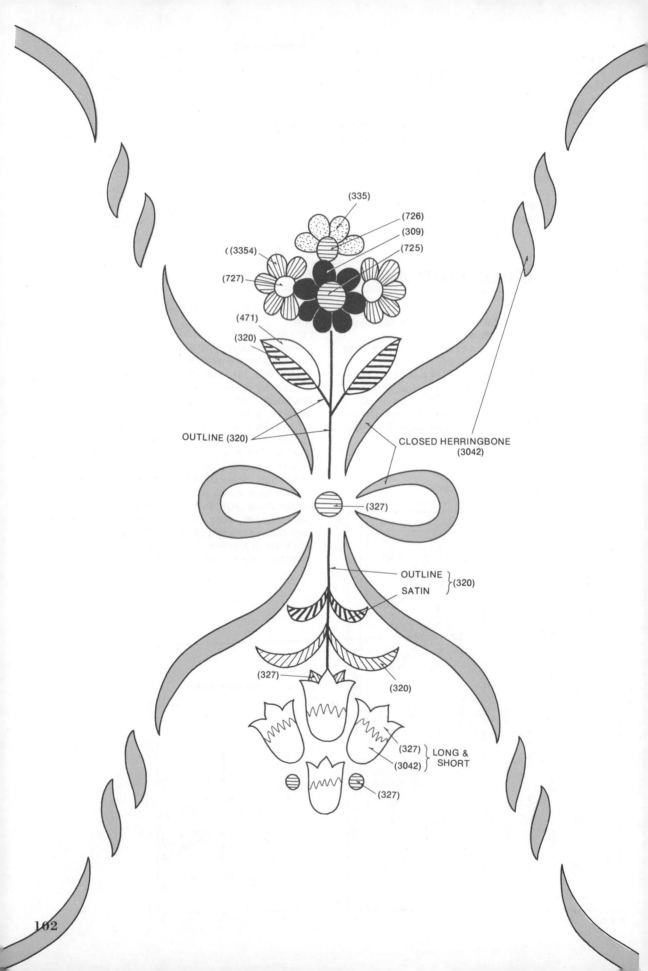

(335)

(726)

(309)

((3354)

(725)

(727)

(471)

(320)

OUTLINE (320)

CLOSED HERRINGBONE
(3042)

(327)

OUTLINE
SATIN } (320)

(327)

(320)

(327) } LONG &
(3042) } SHORT

(327)

BLUE ROSE DOILY AND MATCHING COASTERS shown on page 27

MATERIALS

Fabric: Blue linen, 35 cm square for doily. Blue linen, 15 cm square for one coaster.

Threads: D.M.C. #25 six-strand embroidery floss.

FOR DOILY

1½ skeins of 826 (forget-me-not blue). 1 skein each of 813 (forget-me-not blue) and 992 (peacock green). ½ skein of 993 (peacock green). Small amount each of 827 (forget-me-not blue) and 943 (jade green).

FOR SIX COASTERS

1 skein of 826 (forget-me-not blue). Small amount each of 725, 726 (saffron), 813 (forget-me-not blue), 912, 954 (emerald green), 992 and 993 (peacock green).

FINISHED SIZE: Doily, 28 cm in diameter. Coaster, 11 cm in diameter.

DIRECTIONS: FOR DOILY Trace actual size pattern. Transfer design to fabric with one section following another to make a complete circle (see diagram). Use two strands of floss in needle throughout. Buttonhole stitch along scallop outline. Trim excess fabric beyond stitching. Press. FOR COASTER Trace actual size pattern. Transfer design to fabric. Work in same manner as for doily. Make six coasters, three yellow-range and three blue-range.

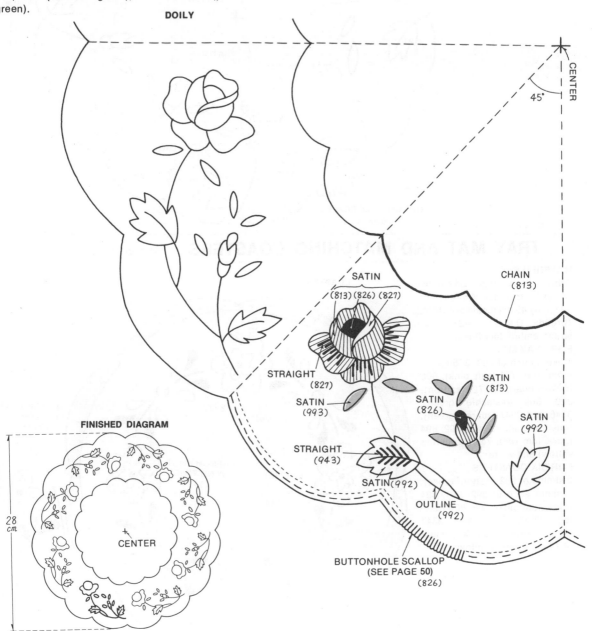

DOILY

FINISHED DIAGRAM

CENTER

28 cm

103

COASTER

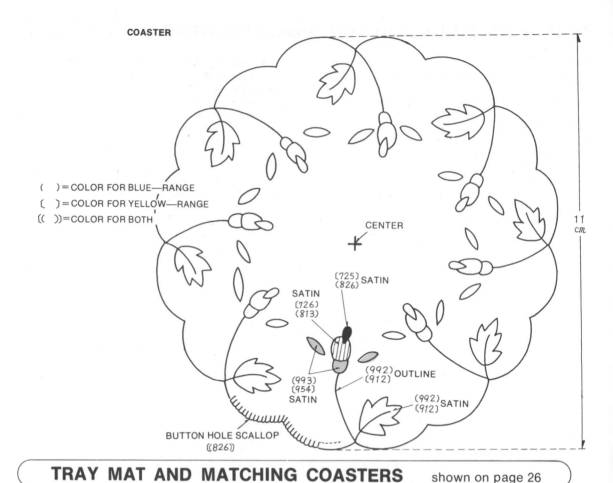

( ) = COLOR FOR BLUE—RANGE
[ ] = COLOR FOR YELLOW—RANGE
(( )) = COLOR FOR BOTH

CENTER

(725) (826) SATIN

SATIN (726) (813)

(992) (912) OUTLINE

(993) (954) SATIN

(992) (912) SATIN

BUTTON HOLE SCALLOP ((826))

11 cm

TRAY MAT AND MATCHING COASTERS shown on page 26

MATERIALS

Fabric: White linen, 34 cm by 48 cm for tray mat. White linen, 30 cm by 45 cm for six coasters.
Threads: D.M.C. #25 six-strand embroidery floss.

FOR TRAY MAT

1 skein each of 309, 335 (geranium red), 776 (soft pink), 800 (Sèvres blue), 725, 726 (saffron), 320, 368 (pistachio green), 3346 and 3347 (scarab green). Small amount each of 892, 894 (geranium red), 743 (tangerine yellow) and white.

FOR SIX COASTERS

2 skeins of 963 (magenta rose). 1 skein each of 892, 891, 894 (geranium pink), 798, 800 (Sèvres blue), 3346 and 3347 (scarab green). Small amount of 743 (tangerine yellow).

COASTER

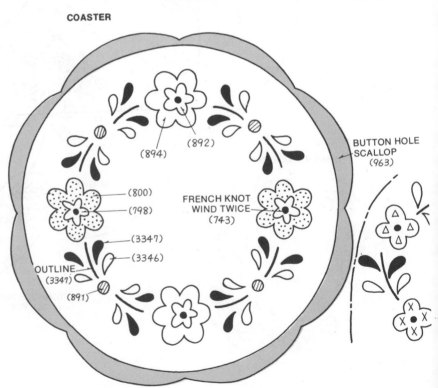

(892)

(894)

(800)

(798)

(3347)

(3346)

FRENCH KNOT WIND TWICE (743)

OUTLINE (3347)

(891)

BUTTON HOLE SCALLOP (963)

104

FINISHED SIZE: Tray mat, 30 cm by 44 cm. Coaster, 9.7 cm in diameter.

DIRECTIONS: FOR TRAY MAT Trace actual size pattern. Transfer design to fabric, reversing design for left side and top half (see diagram). Work all embroidery in satin stitch with two strands of floss in needle unless otherwise indicated. When embroidery is finished, pull out two threads of fabric 3.2 cm from edges. Fold edges 0.8 cm all around to back and refold 1.2 cm. Hem stitch with two strands of floss in white. Press. FOR COASTER Trace actual size pattern. Transfer design to fabric. Work in same manner as for tray mat. Buttonhole stitch along scallop outline. Trim fabric beyond stitching. Press.

TRAY MAT

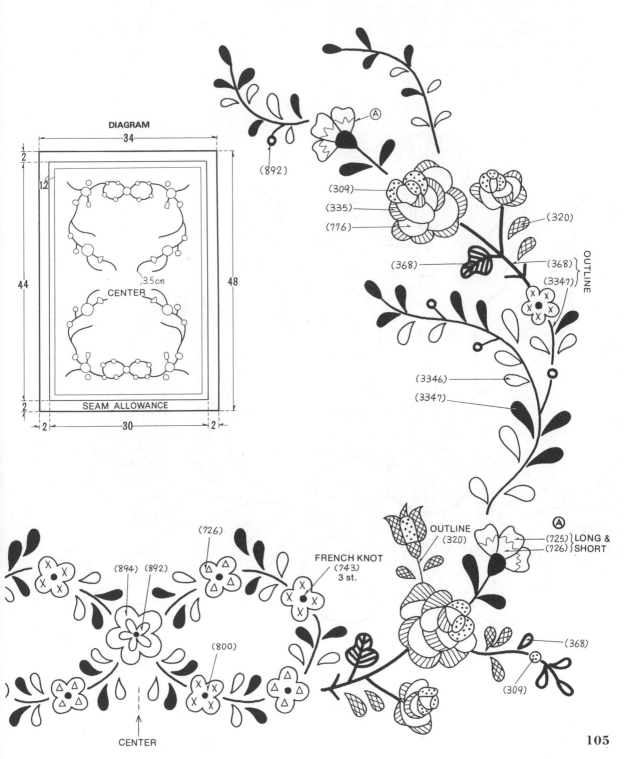

105

WHITE FLOWERED TABLE CENTER AND DOILIES shown on page 28

TABLE CENTER
MATERIALS
Fabric: Powder green linen, 65 cm by 130 cm.
Threads: D.M.C. #25 six-strand embroidery floss.
14 skeins of white.
FINISHED SIZE: 61 cm in diameter.
DIRECTIONS: Cut fabric with seam allowances
referring to diagram. Trace actual size pattern.
Transfer design to fabric. Using two strands of floss
in needle, work as indicated. With right sides of
embroidered piece and border together, stitch
around edges. Turn right side out. Outline stitch
along seam line with three strands of floss in needle.
Finish edge with narrow hem. Press.

DETAILS OF EYELET HOLE

PADDED
SATIN

OUTLINE

EYELET HOLE.

CHAIN

TRELLIS STITCH
1 st.

OUTLINE 3 st.

FINISHED DIAGRAM

BORDER FABRIC

CENTER

60°

11.5cm

3.5cm

OUTLINE

61cm

DETAILS OF TRELLIS STITCH
(Draw out every 3rd & 4th thread leaving threads 1, 2, 5, 6......etc. in both vertical & horizontal directions)

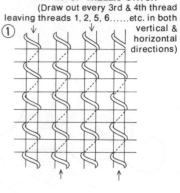

①

②

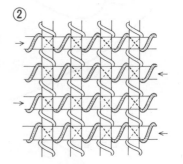

DOILIES
MATERIALS
Fabric: Powder green linen, 80 cm by 40 cm for left side doily. Powder green linen, 50 cm by 25 cm for right side doily.
Threads: D.M.C. #25 six-strand embroidery floss.

5 skeins of white for left side doily. 2 skeins of white for right side doily.
FINISHED SIZE: Left side doily, 36 cm in diameter. Right side doily, 23 cm in diameter.
DIRECTIONS: Work in same manner as for table center.

LEFT SIDE

PADDED SATIN   EYELET HOLE

OUTLINE

CHAIN

TRELLIS STITCH 1 st.

OUTLINE 3 st.

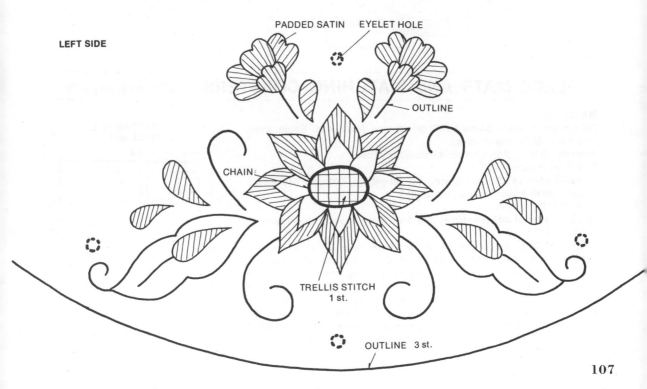

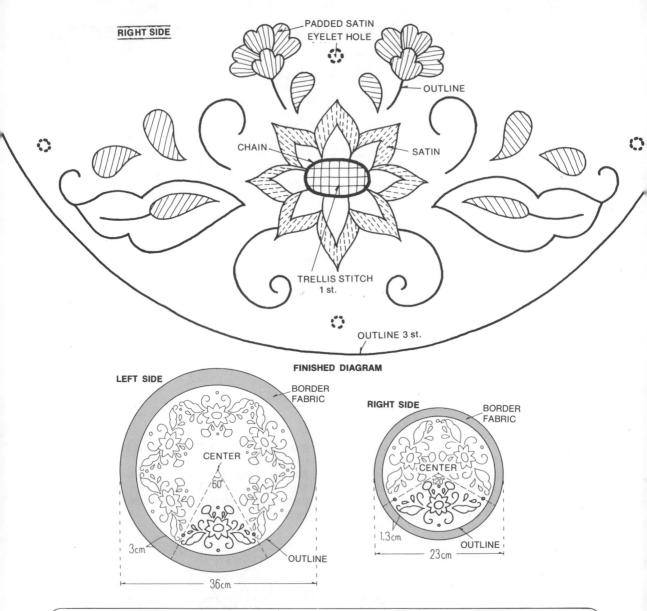

RIGHT SIDE

PADDED SATIN
EYELET HOLE

OUTLINE

CHAIN

SATIN

TRELLIS STITCH
1 st.

OUTLINE 3 st.

FINISHED DIAGRAM

LEFT SIDE

BORDER
FABRIC

CENTER

60°

3cm

OUTLINE

36cm

RIGHT SIDE

BORDER
FABRIC

CENTER

120°

1.3cm

OUTLINE

23cm

PLACE MATS AND MATCHING COASTERS   shown on page 29

MATERIALS

Fabric: Beige linen, 54 cm by 33 cm for one place mat. Beige linen, 15 cm square for one coaster.

Threads: D.M.C. # 25 six-strand embroidery floss.

FOR ONE PLACE MAT

½ skein each of 632 (chocolate), 407 (chestnut), 842 and 840 (beige brown). Small amount of 950 (chestnut).

FOR ONE COASTER

½ skein each of 407 (chestnut) and 840 (beige brown). Small amount of 842 (beige brown).

FINISHED SIZE: Place mat, 50 cm by 29 cm. Coaster, 12 cm square.

DIRECTIONS: FOR PLACE MAT Trace actual size pattern. Transfer design to both sides of fabric (see diagram). Using two strands of floss in needle, work as indicated. When embroidery is finished, pull out two threads of fabric 3.2 cm from edges. Fold edges 0.8 cm all around to back and refold 1.2 cm. Hem stitch inner edges to pulled thread line, with single strand of 842 (beige brown). Press. FOR COASTER Trace actual size pattern. Transfer design to fabric. Work in same manner as for place mat.

DIAGRAM FOR
PLACE MAT

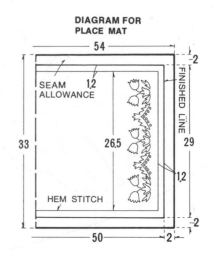

54

2

SEAM
ALLOWANCE

1.2

FINISHED LINE

33

26.5

29

1.2

HEM STITCH

2

50

2

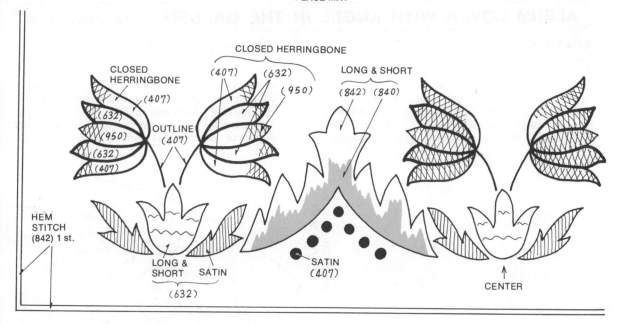

CLOSED HERRINGBONE

CLOSED
HERRINGBONE
(407)

(407) (632)

(950)

LONG & SHORT
(842) (840)

(632)
(950)
(632)
(407)

OUTLINE
(407)

HEM
STITCH
(842) 1 st.

LONG &
SHORT

SATIN

SATIN
(407)

CENTER

(632)

COASTER

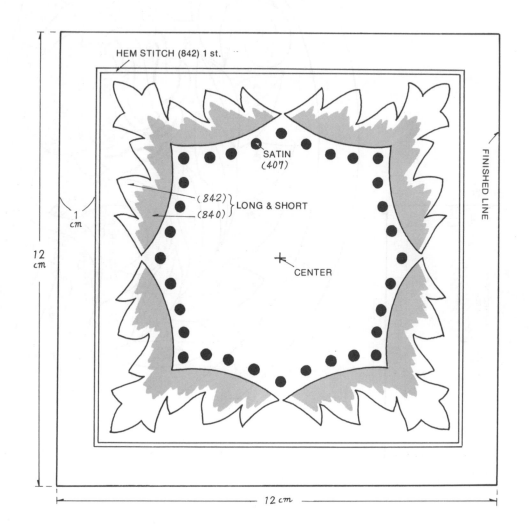

HEM STITCH (842) 1 st.

SATIN
(407)

(842)
(840)

LONG & SHORT

CENTER

FINISHED LINE

1
cm

12
cm

12 cm

ALBUM COVER WITH ANGEL IN THE GARDEN

shown on page 30

MATERIALS

Fabric: Green velveteen for cover, 45 cm by 94 cm. Beige silk for embroidery, 32 cm by 25 cm.

Threads: D.M.C. #25 six-strand embroidery floss. 1 skein each of 754, 948 (geranium red), 3011, 3012 and 3013 (sage green). ½ skein each of 950 (chestnut), 353 (geranium red), 937, 469, 470, 471, 472 (moss green), 3052 (green), 580, 581 (golden green), 989 (laurel green), 680 (old gold), 309, 335 (garnet red), 961, 962, 963 (magenta rose), 3689 (raspberry red), 928 (myrtle grey), 434, 435 and 437 (umber). Small amount each of 761 (morocco red), 3051, 3053 (green), 367 (indigo), 320 (pistachio green), 732, 733, 734 (yellow green), 832, 833 (copper green), 729 (old gold), 783 (golden yellow), 613 (drab), 422 (hazel-nut brown), 644 (smoke grey), 326, 350

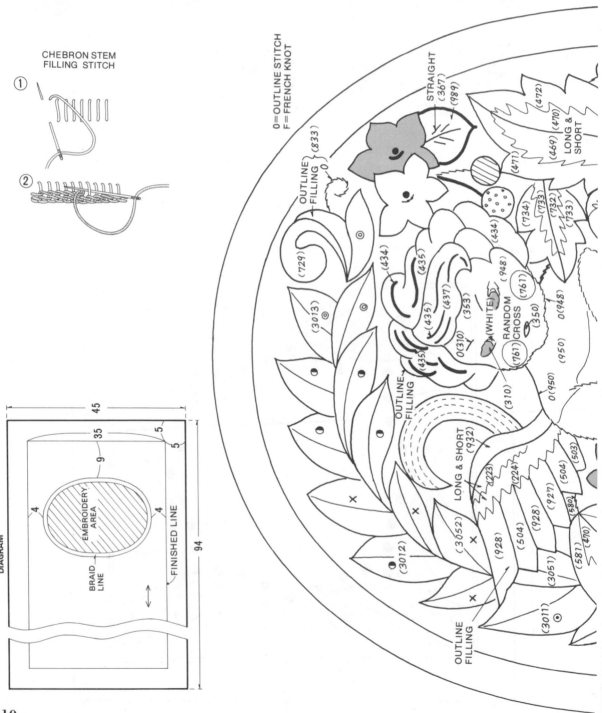

CHEBRON STEM
FILLING STITCH

O=OUTLINE STITCH
F=FRENCH KNOT

DIAGRAM

(geranium red), 3685, 3687, 3688 (raspberry red), 355, 356, 758 (terra-cotta), 927 (myrtle grey), 503, 504 (almond green), 932 (antique blue), 725 (saffron), 3350 (old rose), 223, 224 (faded pink), 310 (black) and white.

Golden braid, 1 cm by 75 cm.

FINISHED SIZE: 40 cm by 35 cm.

DIRECTIONS: Trace actual size pattern. Transfer design to center of beige silk. Work all embroidery in satin stitch with two strands of floss in needle unless otherwise indicated. When embroidery is finished, press. Cut oval out of velveteen 1 cm inside inner edge of braid line. Clip into edge all around. Turn clipped edges to back. Place embroidered piece behind cut away velveteen. Slip stitch neatly. Place braid along seam line and slip stitch. You may need a professional help for a finished album.

S=SATIN STITCH
St=STRAIGHT STITCH
OF=OUTLINE FILLING STITCH

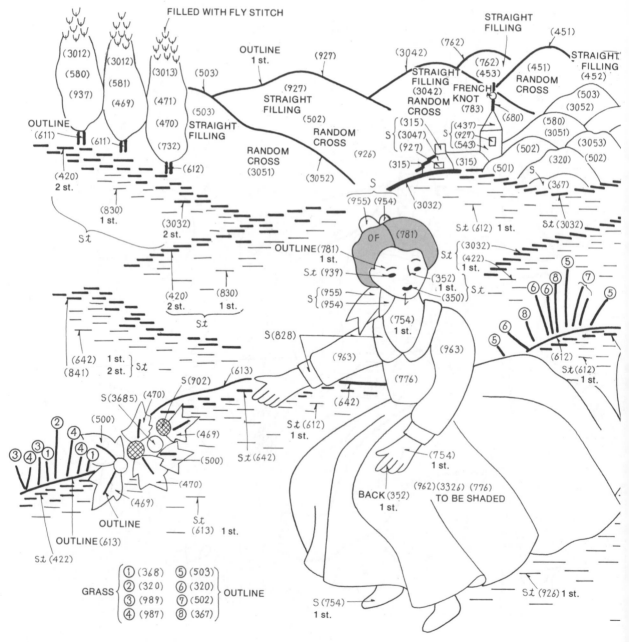

FILLED WITH FLY STITCH

(3012)
(580)
(937)

(3012)
(581)
(469)

(3013)
(471)
(470)
(732)

(503)
(503)

OUTLINE
1 st.

(927)

(927)
STRAIGHT
FILLING
(502)
RANDOM
CROSS
(926)

STRAIGHT
FILLING

RANDOM
CROSS
(3051)

(3052)

(3042)
(762)
(762)
(453)

STRAIGHT
FILLING
(3042)
RANDOM
CROSS

STRAIGHT
FILLING

FRENCH
KNOT
(783)

(451)
(451)
RANDOM
CROSS

STRAIGHT
FILLING
(452)

(503)
(3052)
(580)
(3051)
(3053)
(502)

OUTLINE
(611)

(611)

STRAIGHT
FILLING

S {(315) (3047) (927)

(315)

(680)

S {(437) (927) (543)

(315)

(502)
(320)
(367)

(612)

(420)
2 st.

(830)
1 st.

(3032)
2 st.

St

(501)
(3032)

S (955) (954)

(3032)

St (612) 1 st.

S

St (3032)

OUTLINE (781)
1 st.
St (939)

St {(3032) (422) 1 st.

(5)

OF (781)

St {(422) 1 st.

S {(955) (954)

(352)
1 st. } St
(350)

(6) (6)

(8)

(7)

(5)

(420)
2 st.

(830)
1 st.

St

(754)
1 st.

(8)

(642) 1 st.
(841) 2 st. } St

S (828)

(963)

(963)

(6)

St

(5)

S (902)

(613)

(776)

(612)
St (612)
1 st.

S (3685) (470)
(500)

(469)

(642)

St (612)
1 st.

(2)
(4)
(4)
(1)

(500)

St (642)

(3) (4) (1)

(470)

(469)

(754)
1 st.

OUTLINE

St
(613) 1 st.

BACK (352)
1 st.

(962)(3326) (776)
TO BE SHADED

OUTLINE (613)

St (422)

GRASS {
(1) (368)   (5) (503)
(2) (320)   (6) (320)
(3) (989)   (7) (502)
(4) (987)   (8) (367)
} OUTLINE

S (754)
1 st.

St (926) 1 st.

FILLED WITH
FEATHER STITCH

(470)

(469)

(3052)

(3052)

(3051)

(3051)

(581)

(470)

(469)

(3052)

(3051)

(422)

(470)

(469)

(3052)

(580)

(469)

(610)

(831)

(422)

(469)

(640)

(612)

OF

OUTLINE (501)

(610)

(3051)

(829)

(3023)

(451)
1 st. } St

CHAIN
FILLING
(676)

(597)
(598) } S

PETAL
BULLION ROSE { (3688)
(3689)

CLOSED
HERRING
BONE (368)

(320)

(367)

(841)
1 st.

OF (841)

FRENCH KNOT (783) 3 st.
PISTIL

(435)
1 st.

OF (435)

(3052)

St (3022)

(320)

S (502)

S { (3042)
(3041)
1 st.

(320)

(368)

(642)

(320)
(3052)
(501)
(937)

(761)
1 st.

(434)

(435)

St

CLOSED
CRETAN

(834)

S
(3072)

S
(778)

(754)
1 st.

(435)
St (3052)
1 st.

St (3052)
1 st.

(503)

(320)

(502)

(841)
1 st.

(320)

S { (469)
(470)

(224)
(223)

(223)

(224)

(225)

(813)

(320)

(316)

S (3685)

(435)
St

(350)

(356)

S (3072)

S (746)

(420)
1 st.

S { (902)
(742)

(761)

1 st.

(827)

(813)

(813)

OF (434)

St
(642)

RUNNING
(3685) 1 st.

(932) (597) (598)

(221) (223) (224) (778)

RUNNING
(433)
1 st.

CLOSED HERRINGBONE
(434)   (435)

(729)

OF (435)

(677)

(676)

CLOSED HERRINGBONE
(729)

S (452)

(676)

452) (453)

S

St (927) 1st.

S (433)

S (937)

S (470)

OF (434)

OUTLINE
(611)

FLOWER { PETAL -- S { O (743)
V (309)
X (962)
△ (3326)
PISTIL
FRENCH KNOT (472)

113

MATERIALS

Fabric: Grey silk pongee, 90 cm by 39 cm.

Threads: D.M.C. #25 six-strand embroidery floss. 1 skein each of 598 (greenish grey), 3326, 776 (soft pink), 469, 470 (moss green), 224 (faded pink), 3051 and 3052 (green). ½ skein each of 597 (greenish grey), 781 (golden yellow), 754 (geranium red), 813, 827, 828 (forget-me-not blue), 962, 963 (magenta rose), 676, 677 (old gold), 841 (beige brown), 761 (morocco red), 3072 (silver grey), 221, 223 (faded pink), 778 (dull mauve), 435 (umber), 3042 (Indian red), 642 (smoke grey), 3032 (dark brown), 612 (drab), 937 (moss green) 3023 (beige), 451, 452 (seagull grey), 580, 581 (golden green), 926, 927 (myrtle grey), 502, 503 (almond green), 320, 367,

368 (pistachio green), 3012, 3013 (sage green), 420, 422 (hazel-nut brown), 613 (brown) and 830 (copper green). Small amount each of 954, 955 (emerald green), 783 (golden yellow), 939 (indigo), 350, 352 (geranium red), 309 (garnet red), 3685, 3688, 3689 (raspberry red), 987, 989 (laurel green), 471, 472 (moss green), 902 (scarlet), 742, 743 (tangerine yellow), 356 (terra-cotta), 433, 434, 437 (umber), 225 (faded pink) 315, 316 (dull mauve), 3041 (Indian red), 746, 3053 (green), 932 (antique blue), 829, 831, 834 (copper green), 680, 729 (old gold), 610, 611 (drab), 640 (smoke grey), 453 (seagull grey), 762 (ash grey), 500, 501 (ivy green), 732 (yellow green), 543 (beige brown), 3022 and 3047 (beige).

FINISHED SIZE: 38 cm by 29 cm.

DIRECTIONS: Trace actual size pattern. Transfer design to fabric. Work all embroidery in long and short stitch with two strands of floss in needle unless otherwise indicated. Note that skirts of three girls are to be shaded. You may need a professional help for a finished album.

DIAGRAM

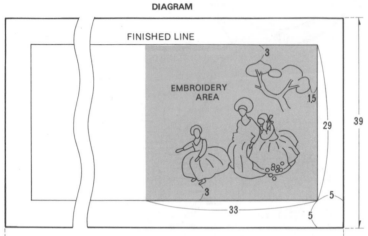

SACHET   shown on page 32

MATERIALS

Fabric: Pink silk satin, 24 cm by 23 cm.

Threads: D.M.C. #25 six-strand embroidery floss. ½ skein each of 956, 957 (peony rose), 893, 894 (geranium pink), 605 (cerise), 776, 899 (soft pink), 335 (garnet red), 352 (geranium red), 760, 761 (morocco red), 368 (pistachio green), 912, 955

(emerald green), 993 (peacock green), 989 (laurel green), 813 and 826 (forget-me-not blue). Small amount each of 351, 353, 891 (geranium red), 963 (magenta rose), 309, 326 (garnet red), 3326 (soft pink), 600 (cerise), 743, 744 (tangerine yellow) and 3078 (light yellow).

Salmon pink ribbon, 2.5 cm by 75 cm. Small amount of potpourri-dried mixed flower.

FINISHED SIZE: See diagram.

DIRECTIONS: Trace actual size pattern. Transfer design to fabric. Work all embroidery in long and short stitch with two strands of floss in needle unless otherwise indicated. When embroidery is finished, run a gathering stitch in place. With right sides together, stitch along long edges to make tube. Bring seamline to center of tube and stitch across bottom 1 cm from raw edges. Press. Turn right side out and fill potpourri. Turn 1 cm inside at the top and slip stitch. Pull both ends of gathering thread as shown in diagram. Sew ribbon in place.

DIAGRAM

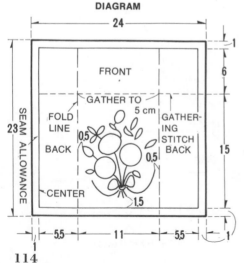

FINISHED DIAGRAM

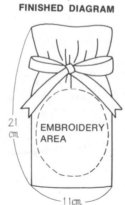

114

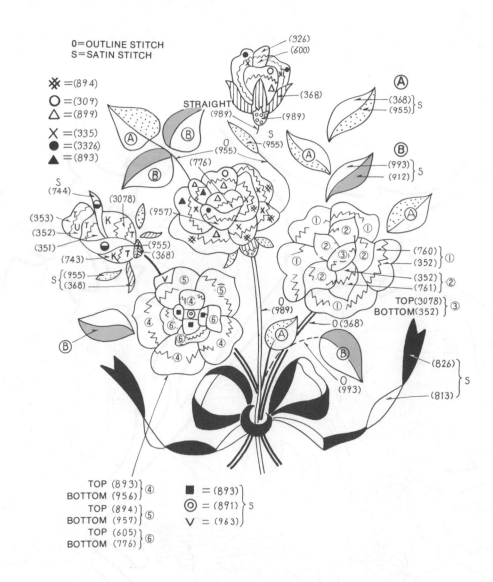

O=OUTLINE STITCH
S=SATIN STITCH

✳ =(894)
O =(309)
△ =(899)
X =(335)
● =(3326)
▲ =(893)

(326)
(600)

STRAIGHT
(989)

(368)

(955)

Ⓐ (368)
(955) } S

S
(955)

O
(955)

(776)

Ⓑ (993)
(912) } S

Ⓐ

S
(744)

(3078)

(957)

(353)
(352)
(351)

Ⓐ

(743)

(955)
(368)

S { (955)
(368)

(760)
(352) } ①

(352)
(761) } ②

TOP (3078)
BOTTOM (352) } ③

O
(989)

O(368)

O
(993)

(826)
(813) } S

TOP (893)
BOTTOM (956) } ④

■ = (893)
◎ = (891)
V = (963) } S

TOP (894)
BOTTOM (957) } ⑤

TOP (605)
BOTTOM (776) } ⑥

ALBUM COVER WITH ARABESQUE DESIGN shown on page 31, bottom

MATERIALS
Fabric: Beige silk, 45 cm by 94 cm.
Threads: D.M.C. #25 six-strand embroidery floss.
2 skeins of 517 (sky blue). 1 skein each of 3326 (soft
pink), 518 (sky blue), 436, 738 (umber), and 919 (red
brown). ½ skein each of 3350 (old rose), 335 (garnet
red), 469 (moss green), 921 (red brown), 221, 223,
224 (faded pink), 315 and 778 (dull mauve). Small
amount each of 470, 471 (moss green), 747 (sky
blue), 920, 922 (red brown) and 309 (garnet red).
FINISHED SIZE: 40 cm by 35 cm.
DIRECTIONS: Trace actual size pattern. Transfer
design to fabric reversing design for other half. Work
all embroidery in satin stitch with two strands of
floss in needle unless otherwise indicated. You may
need a professional help for a finished album.

DIAGRAM

FINISHED LINE

1cm

3 cm

35

45

1cm

5

5

94

CENTER →

F

OUTLINE (517)

C

C

LONG & SHORT

LONG & SHORT (517)

A

A

(3326)
(335)
(3350)

(3326)

CHAIN (517)

E

CHAIN (919)

T T T T
X
X
X X
T T

LONG & SHORT (518)
OUTLINE

B

B

E

(517)
(518)
(471)
(747)

OUTLINE (224)
(315)
(469)
(778)
(223)
(309)

E

X

EVENING BAG AND MATCHING TISSUE CASE shown on page 32

MATERIALS

Fabric: Blue grey silk satin, 37 cm by 45 cm for evening bag. Blue grey silk satin, 30 cm by 13 cm for tissue case. Grey bemberg for lining, 37 cm by 22 cm for evening bag. Frey bemberg for lining, 18 cm by 13 cm for tissue case.

Threads: D.M.C. #25 six-strand embroidery floss.
FOR EVENING BAG
½ skein each of 834 (copper green), 699 (brilliant green), 353 (geranium red), 894 (geranium pink). Small amount each of 436 (umber), 995, 996, 797 (royal blue), 798, 800 (Sèvres blue), 972 (canary yellow), 740, 741, 743 (tangerine yellow), 911, 912, 913 (emerald green), 891, 893 (geranium pink), 309, 335 (garnet red), 776, 818, 899 (soft pink), 962, 963 (magenta rose), 498 (scarlet), 352, 353, 754, 948 (geranium red), 988 (laurel green), 3347 (scarab green), 470, 472 (moss green), 954, 955 (emerald green), 368 (pistachio green), 602 and 604 (cerise).

FOR TISSUE CASE
½ skein of 834 (copper green). Small amount each of 436 (umber), 891, 893, 894 (geranium pink), 954 and 955 (emerald green).

Grey silk cord for evening bag, 0.5 cm in diameter and 120 cm long. Cardboard, 14.5 cm by 11 cm.
FINISHED SIZE: See diagram.
DIRECTIONS: FOR EVENING BAG Trace actual size pattern. Transfer design to fabric. Work in long and short stitch with two strands of floss in needle unless otherwise indicated. Press, when embroidery is finished. Join embroidered piece and lining. Stitch side seam to make tube. Sew outer bottom piece in place. Cover two pieces of cardboard with grey bemberg. Slip stitch to wrong side of bottom. Turn right side out. Attach thread carriers in place. Slip two 60 cm length of cords through carriers from both sides. Tie ends. FOR TISSUE CASE Trace actual size pattern. Transfer design to fabric, reversing design for opposite side. Work in satin and outline stitches with two strands of floss in needle throughout. Cut two strips of 2 cm by 12.5 cm on the bias from silk satin. Incase both shorter edges of outer fabric and lining together in bias binding. Bring folded edges to center and stitch across top and bottom with right sides together. Turn inside out.

EVENING BAG

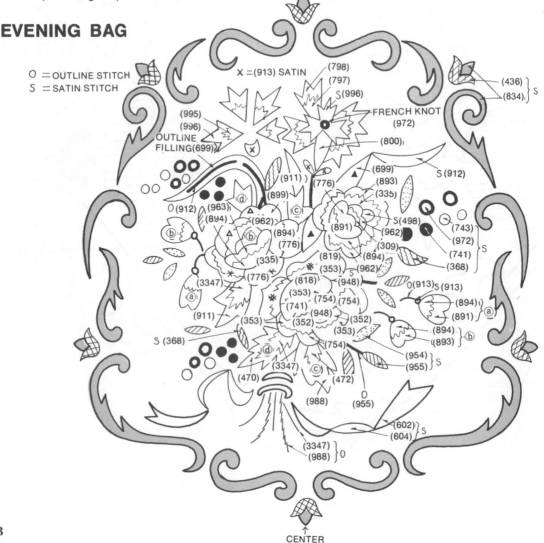

118

CENTER

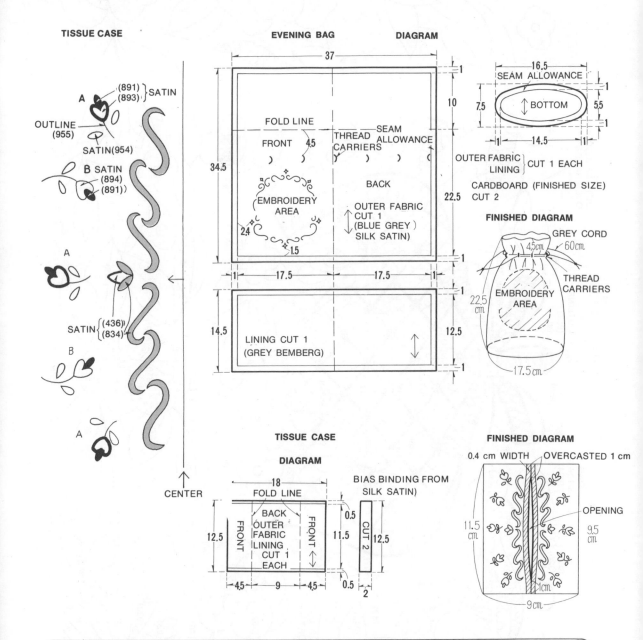

FLOWER BASKET JEWELRY BOX shown on page 33

MATERIALS

Fabric: Ivory silk, 35 cm by 20 cm.

Threads: D.M.C. #25 six-strand embroidery floss. ½ skein each of 3685, 3687, 3688, 3689 (raspberry red), 550 (plum), 327 (violet mauve), 3042 (Indian red), 892, 894 (geranium pink), 921, 922 (red brown), 309, 326, 335 (garnet red), 957 (peony rose), 776 (soft pink), 350, 351, 352 (geranium red), 761 (morocco red), 832, 834 (copper green), 319, 320, 367, 368 (pistachio green), 469 (moss green), 504 (almond green) and 597 (greenish grey). Small amount each of 718, 917 (episcopal purple), 891 (geranium pink), 776, 818, 819, 899 (soft pink), 956 (peony rose), 725, 726, 727 (saffron), 3078 (light yellow), 972 (canary yellow), 920 (red brown), 828 (forget-me-not blue), 470, 471, 472 (moss green),

369 (pistachio green), 991 (peacock green), 913 (emerald green), 501 (ivy green), 502 and 503 (almond green).

Unfinished jewelry box (as for the shape, see photograph).

FINISHED SIZE: 28.5 cm by 13.5 cm (embroidery area).

DIRECTIONS: Trace actual size pattern. Transfer design to fabric. Work all embroidery in satin stitch with two strands of floss in needle unless otherwise indicated. When embroidery is finished, press. You may need a professional help for a finished jewelry box.

119

120

MATERIALS
Fabric: Navy blue cotton satin, 20 cm by 11 cm.
Threads: D.M.C. #25 six-strand embroidery floss. ½ skein each of 604 (cerise), 798 (Sèvres blue), 943 (jade green) and 992 (peacock green). Small amount each of 601, 602, 603 (cerise), 792 (cornflower blue), 700 (brilliant green), 954 (emerald green), 991 (peacock green) and 743 (tangerine yellow).
FINISHED SIZE: 18 cm by 9.5 cm.
DIRECTIONS: Trace actual size pattern. Transfer design to fabric. Work in satin stitch with two strands of floss in needle unless otherwise indicated. When embroidery is finished, press. You may need a professional help for a finished glasses case.

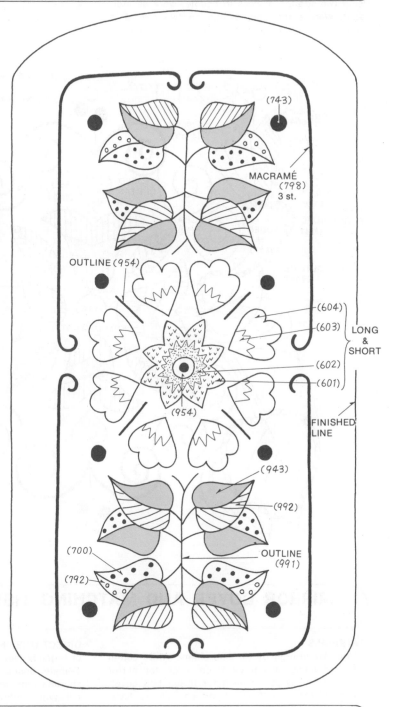

MATERIALS
Fabric: Beige silk satin, 40 cm by 20 cm.
Threads: D.M.C. #25 six-strand embroidery floss. 1 skein each of 552 (plum) and 718 (episcopal purple). ½ skein each of 601, 603, 604 (cerise), 703 (brilliant green), 905, 907 (parakeet green), 783 (golden yellow), 991, 993 (peacock green) and 996 (royal blue). Small amount each of 311, 312 (indigo), 307 (lemon yellow), 444 (buttercup yellow), 725, 726 (saffron), 791, 792 (cornflower blue), 3345, 3347 and 3348 (scarab green).
Unfinished sewing box, 35 cm wide ×17.5 cm long ×19 cm high. As for the shape, see photograph.
FINISHED SIZE: 13.5 cm square (embroidery area).

121

DIRECTIONS: Cut two pieces of 20 cm square. Trace actual size pattern. Transfer design to fabric. Using two strands of floss in needle, work as indicated. Work embroidery design on two pieces in same manner. You may need a professional help for a finished sewing box.

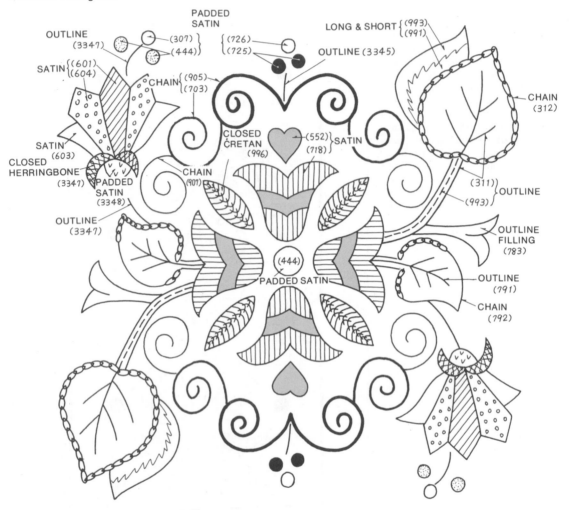

MIRROR COVER AND MATCHING TISSUE BOX COVER
shown on page 34, top

MATERIALS

Fabric: White organdy for embroidery. White cotton lawn for lining. 40 cm by 20 cm each for mirror cover. 90 cm by 20 cm each for tissue box cover.

Threads: D.M.C. #25 six-strand embroidery floss.

FOR MIRROR COVER
1 skein each of 818, 899 (soft pink) and 957 (peony rose).

FOR TISSUE BOX COVER
1 skein each of 818 (soft pink), and 957 (peony rose).
½ skein of 899 (soft pink).
Soft pink bias binding, 90 cm long. Crochet-type white lace, 1 cm by 220 cm.

FINISHED SIZE: Mirror cover, 17.5 cm in diameter. Tissue box cover, see diagram.

DIRECTIONS: FOR MIRROR COVER Cut two pieces of organdy (see diagram). Trace actual size pattern. Transfer design to fabric. Work in shadow and satin stitches with two strands of floss in needle throughout. Work embroidery design on two pieces in same manner. Pin embroidered piece against right side of lawn. Baste along cutting line. Cut out circle of 17.5 cm in diameter. With linings facing, incase raw edges of top half in bias binding. For buttom half, incase front and back edges indivisually in bias binding. Make two 14 cm length of strips of bias binding. Tie into bow each and sew them in place. FOR TISSUE BOX COVER Place white organdy against cotton lawn and cut together as indicated (see diagram). Trace actual size pattern.

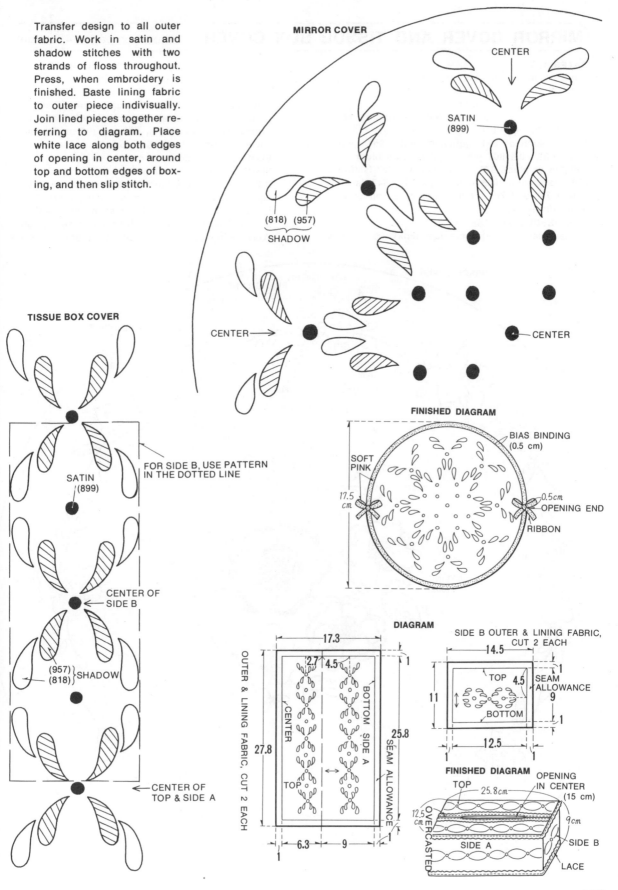

Transfer design to all outer fabric. Work in satin and shadow stitches with two strands of floss throughout. Press, when embroidery is finished. Baste lining fabric to outer piece indivisually. Join lined pieces together referring to diagram. Place white lace along both edges of opening in center, around top and bottom edges of boxing, and then slip stitch.

MIRROR COVER

CENTER

SATIN (899)

(818) (957)
SHADOW

CENTER

CENTER

FINISHED DIAGRAM

BIAS BINDING (0.5 cm)

SOFT PINK

17.5 cm

0.5cm
OPENING END

RIBBON

TISSUE BOX COVER

FOR SIDE B, USE PATTERN IN THE DOTTED LINE

SATIN (899)

CENTER OF SIDE B

(957)
(818) SHADOW

CENTER OF TOP & SIDE A

DIAGRAM

SIDE B OUTER & LINING FABRIC, CUT 2 EACH

OUTER & LINING FABRIC, CUT 2 EACH

17.3

2.7 4.5

1

CENTER

BOTTOM SIDE A

27.8

25.8

SEAM ALLOWANCE

TOP

6.3

9

1

14.5

1

TOP 4.5

11

SEAM ALLOWANCE

BOTTOM

9

12.5

1

1

1

FINISHED DIAGRAM

TOP

25.8cm

OPENING IN CENTER (15 cm)

12.5 cm

OVERCASTED

SIDE A

9cm

SIDE B

LACE

123

MIRROR COVER AND TISSUE BOX COVER shown on page 34, bottom

MATERIALS

Fabric: Light-weight pink linen. White cotton broadcloth. 40 cm by 20 cm each for mirror cover. 45 cm by 28 cm each for tissue box cover.

Threads: D.M.C. #25 six-strand embroidery floss.
FOR MIRROR COVER
1 skein each of 891 (geranium pink), 957 (peony rose), 601, 602, 604 (cerise), 797 (royal blue), 799, 800 (Sévres blue), 972 (canary yellow), 727 (saffron), 608 (flame red), 988 (laurel green), 3347 (scarab green) 703 and 704 (brilliant green). Small amount of 606 (flame red).

FOR TISSUE BOX CASE
1 skein each of 891 (geranium pink), 957 (peony

rose), 602, 604 (cerise), 550, 552 (plum), 209 (parma violet), 797 (royal blue), 799, 800 (Sèvres blue), 727 (saffron), 741 (tangerine yellow), 608 (flame red), 988 (laurel green), 3347 (scarab green), and 704 (brilliant green). Small amount of 606 (flame red). Crochet-type white lace, 300 cm. (90 cm for mirror cover. 210 cm for tissue box cover.)
Elastic tape, 0.5 cm by 28 cm.

FINISHED SIZE: See diagram.

DIRECTIONS: FOR MIRROR COVER Cut two 20 cm square out of linen. Trace actual size pattern. Transfer design to fabric. Work in satin stitch with one strand of floss in needle unless otherwise indicated. Work embroidery design on two pieces in same

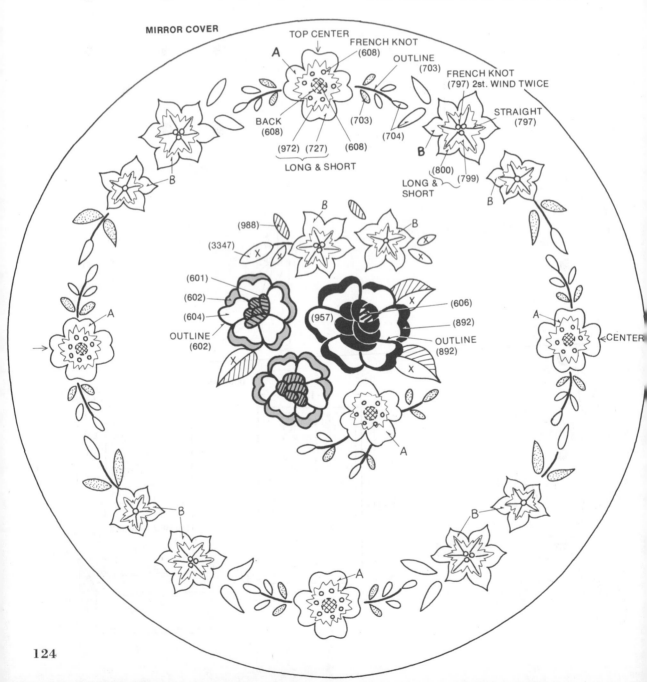

124

manner. Cut out circle 1 cm outside of marked line from embroidered pieces. Cut out circle of same size from broadcloth. With right sides of linen and broadcloth together, stitch around edges leaving 6 cm opening. Turn inside out. Slip stitch opening closed. Repeat for the other side. With linings facing, stitch top half along edges. Place white lace all around front edge and slip stitch in place. Slip stitch white lace to bottom half of back side. FOR TISSUE BOX COVER Cut fabric as indicated in diagram. Trace actual size pattern. Transfer design to fabric, reversing design for opposite side. Work in satin stitch with one strand of floss in needle unless otherwise indicated. Join boxing pieces and embroidered pieces together with folded edges meeting in center of top. Join lining fabric in same manner. With linings facing, stitch along top and bottom folded edges. Overcast both ends of center opening 3.5 cm from each end. Place white lace along both edges of opening in center, around top and bottom edges of boxing and slip stitch. Sew elastic tape in place at the bottom.

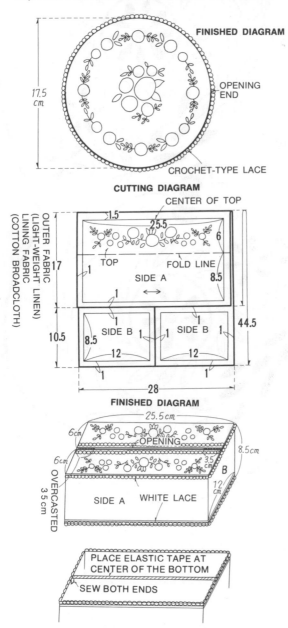

FINISHED DIAGRAM

17.5 cm

OPENING END

CROCHET-TYPE LACE

CUTTING DIAGRAM

Outer Fabric (LIGHT-WEIGHT LINEN)
Lining Fabric (COTTON BROADCLOTH)

CENTER OF TOP

1.5   25.5   6
TOP   FOLD LINE
17   1   SIDE A   8.5
1
1   1   1   1
10.5   SIDE B   SIDE B   44.5
8.5   1   1
12   12
1   1
28

FINISHED DIAGRAM

25.5 cm
6 cm   OPENING   8.5 cm
6 cm   3.5 cm   B
OVERCASTED 3.5 cm   12 cm
SIDE A   WHITE LACE

PLACE ELASTIC TAPE AT CENTER OF THE BOTTOM
SEW BOTH ENDS

TISSUE BOX COVER

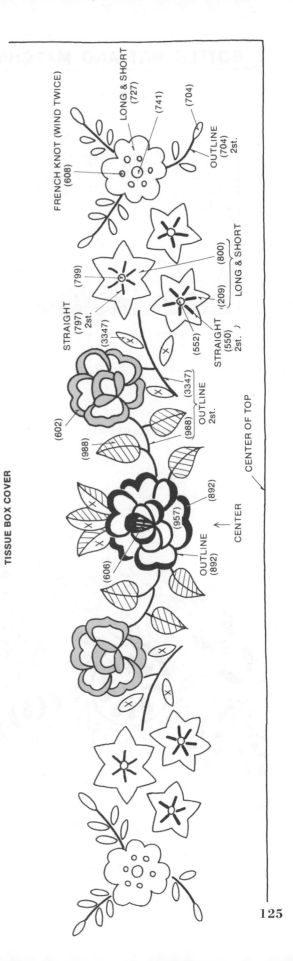

FRENCH KNOT (WIND TWICE) (608)

LONG & SHORT (727)

(741)

(704)

OUTLINE (704) 2st.

STRAIGHT (797) 2st.

(799)

(800)

(209)   LONG & SHORT

(552)

STRAIGHT (550) 2st.

STRAIGHT (550) 2st.

(3347)

(3347)

OUTLINE (988) 2st.

(602)

(988)

CENTER OF TOP

(892)

(957)

CENTER

(606)

OUTLINE (892)

125

BOTTLE MAT AND MATCHING COASTERS

shown on page 35

FINISHED DIAGRAM

MATERIALS

Fabric: Light-weight linen in white and light blue.
30 cm square each for bottle mat. 84 cm by 14 cm in
light blue for six coasters.

28

1.8 cm

1.8 cm

28

CENTER

BOTTLE MAT

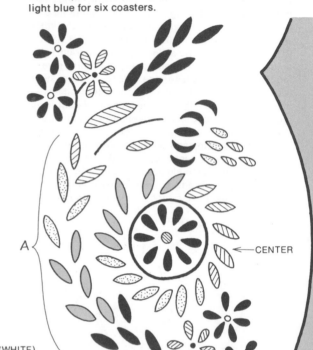

A

CENTER

FABRIC (WHITE)

B

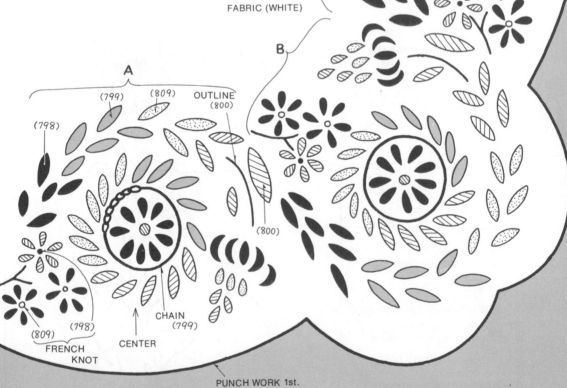

A

(799)

(809)

OUTLINE
(800)

(798)

(800)

(809)   (798)

FRENCH
KNOT

CHAIN
(799)

CENTER

PUNCH WORK 1st.

FABRIC FOR APPLIQUÉ (LIGHT BLUE)

Threads: D.M.C. #25 six-strand embroidery floss. 1 skein each of 798, 799, 800 (Sèvres blue), 809 (forget-me-not blue) and white.

FINISHED SIZE: Bottle mat, 28 cm square. Coaster, 10 cm square.

DIRECTIONS: FOR BOTTLE MAT Trace actual size pattern. Transfer design to fabric, with one section following another. Work in satin stitch with two strands of floss in needle unless otherwise indicated. Cut 0.5 cm inside of marked line out of blue linen with 2 cm seam allowances all around. With right sides of embroidered piece and cut away fabric together, stitch along edges. Clip into edges all around. Turn right side out. Punch work along seam line (see details). Finish edges with narrow hem. Press. FOR COASTER Cut fabric to six pieces of 14 cm square. Trace actual size patterns. Transfer design A to three pieces of fabric, design B to the rest. Work as indicated using two strands of floss in needle throughout. Finish edges with 1 cm hem in outline stitch on right side mitering corners neatly.

COASTER

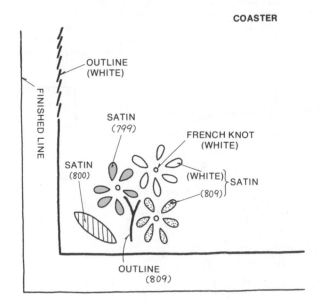

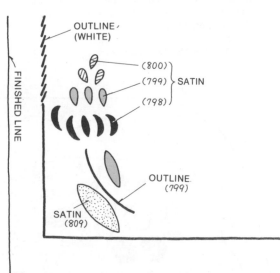

Details of punch work

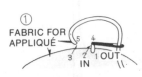

Bring needle out at 1,
in at 2, out at 3.
Then needle returns
to the place where
it came out, in at 2 again (4),
then out at 3 (5).

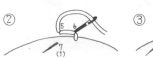

Repeat from 2 to 7.

DIAGRAM

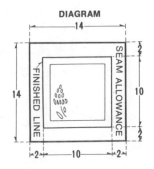

COSMETIC CASE   shown on page 36

MATERIALS

Fabric: Peony rose linen, 35 cm square.
Threads: D.M.C. #25 six-strand embroidery floss. Small amount each of 741 (tangerine yellow), 970, 972 (canary yellow), 704 (brilliant green), 906, 907 (parakeet green), 335 (garnet red), 899, 3326, 776, 818, 819 (soft pink), 891, 893, 894 (geranium pink), 963 (magenta rose), 498 (scarlet), 603 (cerise) 3011 (sage green), 813, 826 (forget-me-not blue), 991, 992 (peacock green), 320, 368, 369 (pistachio green), 581 (golden yellow), 470 (moss green) and 725 (saffron). One zipper, 20 cm long. Iron-on interfacing, 28 cm by 13 cm.
FINISHED SIZE: See diagram.

DIRECTIONS: Cut four pieces for sides and two pieces for gusset with seam allowances out of linen. Cut interfacing to same size as finished case. Trace actual size pattern. Transfer design to two side pieces. Work in long and short stitch with two strands of floss in needle unless otherwise indicated. Work embroidery design on two pieces in same manner. When embroidery is finished, place iron-on interfacing against wrong side of embroidered pieces and outer gusset indivisually. Press. Join outer fabric together. Sew zipper in place. Join inner fabric together. With wrong sides of outer case and inner case together, slip stitch folded edges along zipper.

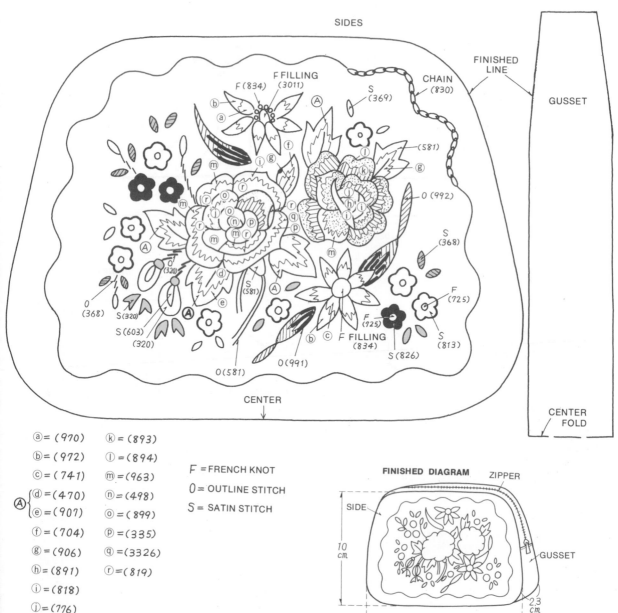

ⓐ = (970) ⓚ = (893)
ⓑ = (972) ⓛ = (894)
ⓒ = (741) ⓜ = (963)
Ⓐ { ⓓ = (470) ⓝ = (498)
     ⓔ = (907) ⓞ = (899)
ⓕ = (704) ⓟ = (335)
ⓖ = (906) ⓠ = (3326)
ⓗ = (891) ⓡ = (819)
ⓘ = (818)
ⓙ = (776)

F = FRENCH KNOT
O = OUTLINE STITCH
S = SATIN STITCH

128

A PAIR OF SLIPPERS shown on page 37, top

MATERIALS

Fabric: Golden brown silk satin, 78 cm by 29 cm.

Threads: D.M.C. # 25 six-strand embroidery floss. ½ skein each of 350 (geranium red), 792, 793 (cornflower blue) and 910 (emerald green). Small amount each of 791 (cornflower blue), 349, 817 (geranium red), 839 (beige brown) and écru.

FINISHED SIZE: Foot size 26 cm.

DIRECTIONS: Cut out two upper pieces and soles each, referring to diagram. Trace actual size pattern. Transfer design to two upper pieces. Using two strands of floss in needle, work as indicated. Machine stitch diagonally across in two directions on two soles. You may need a professional help for a finished slippers.

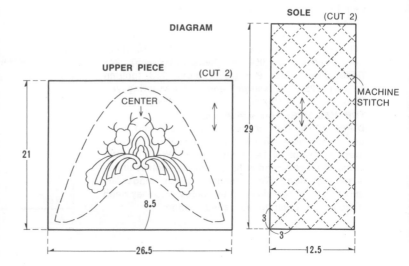

DIAGRAM

UPPER PIECE (CUT 2)

CENTER

21

26.5

8.5

SOLE (CUT 2)

29

MACHINE STITCH

3

3

12.5

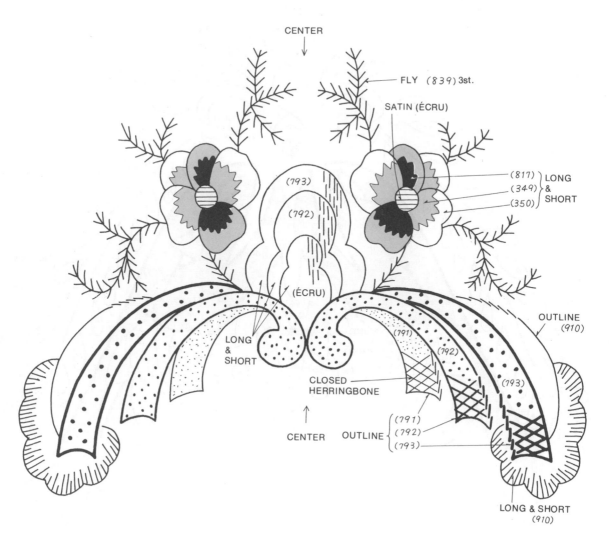

CENTER

FLY (839) 3st.

SATIN (ÉCRU)

(793)

(792)

(817)
(349) } LONG
(350) } & SHORT

(ÉCRU)

LONG & SHORT

OUTLINE (910)

(791)

(792)

CLOSED HERRINGBONE

(793)

CENTER

OUTLINE { (791)
(792)
(793)

LONG & SHORT (910)

129

A PAIR OF SLIPPERS shown on page 37, bottom

MATERIALS

Fabric: Green silk satin, 78 cm by 29 cm.

Threads: D.M.C. #25 six-strand embroidery floss. Small amount each of 905, 906 (parakeet green), 700, 701, 703 (brilliant green), 991, 992, 993 (peacock green), 913, 954, 955 (emerald green), 943 (jade green), 995, 996 (royal blue), 783 (golden yellow), 725, 726 (saffron) and 744 (tangerine yellow).

FINISHED SIZE: Foot size 26 cm.

DIRECTIONS: Cut out two upper pieces and soles each, referring to diagram. Trace actual size pattern. Transfer design to two upper pieces. Work in satin stitch with one strand of floss in needle unless otherwise indicated. Work running stitch diagonally across in two directions on two soles. You may need a professional help for a finished slippers.

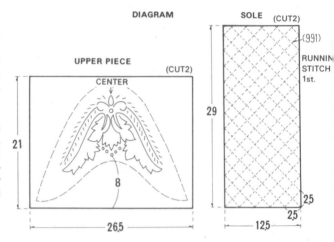

DIAGRAM

UPPER PIECE (CUT2)

CENTER

21

26.5

8

SOLE (CUT2)

(991)

RUNNING STITCH 1st.

29

2.5

2.5

12.5

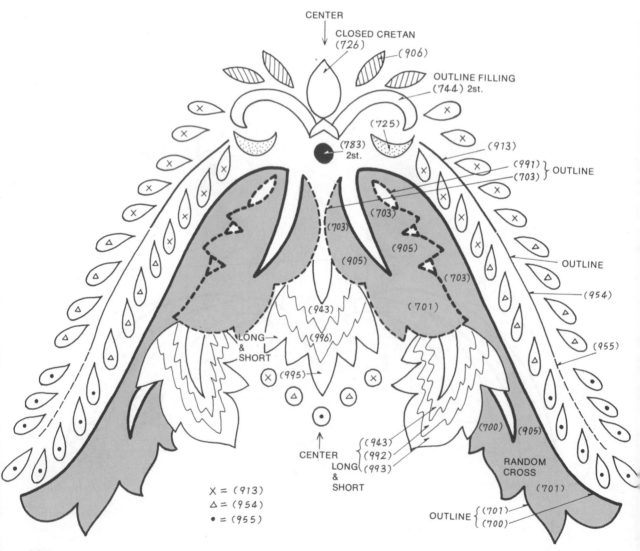

CENTER

CLOSED CRETAN (726)

(906)

OUTLINE FILLING (744) 2st.

(725)

(783) 2st.

(913)

(991) } OUTLINE
(703)

(703)

(703)

(905)

(703)

OUTLINE

(954)

(905)

(701)

(955)

(943)

(996)

LONG & SHORT

(995)

CENTER

(943)
(992)
(993)

LONG & SHORT

(700) (905)

RANDOM CROSS

(701)

X = (913)
△ = (954)
• = (955)

OUTLINE { (701)
(700)

130

BIRD PICTURE

shown on page 38, top

MATERIALS

Fabric: Navy blue linen, 30 cm by 25 cm.

Threads: D.M.C. #25 six-strand embroidery floss. ½ skein each of 3350 (old rose), 224, 225 (faded pink), 975 (umber gold) and 367 (pistachio green). Small amount each of 221, 223 (faded pink), 3687, 3688 (raspberry red), 718 (episcopal purple), 776, 818, 899, 3326 (soft pink), 368 (pistachio green), 989 (laurel green), 780, 782, 783 (golden yellow), 680, 729, 676 (old gold), 725 (saffron), 938 (coffee brown), 351 (geranium red), 741, 743 (tangerine yellow) and écru.

Frame, 24.5 cm by 19.5 cm (inside measurement).

FINISHED SIZE: Same size as frame.

DIRECTIONS: Trace actual size pattern. Transfer design to fabric. Work all embroidery in long and short stitch with two strands of floss in needle unless otherwise indicated. Press, when embroidery is finished. Mount and frame.

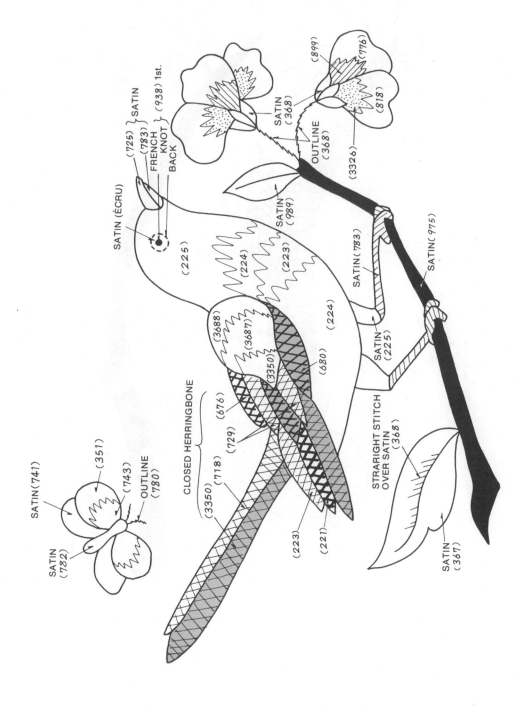

shown on page 38, bottom

MATERIALS

Fabric: Navy blue linen, 30 cm by 25 cm.

Threads: D.M.C. #25 six-strand embroidery floss. ½ skein each of 827, 828 (forget-me-not blue), 988 (laurel green), 975 (umber gold), 943 (jade green) and 995 (royal blue). Small amount each of 813 (forget-me-not blue), 987, 989 (laurel green), 368 (pistachio green), 963 (magenta rose), 783 (golden yellow), 996 (royal blue), 992 (peacock green), 947 (fire red), 938 (coffee brown), 317, 318, 415 (ash grey), 518 (sky blue), écru and white.

Frame, 24.5 cm by 19.5 cm (inside measurement).

FINISHED SIZE: Same size as frame.

DIRECTIONS: Work in same manner as indicated on page 131.

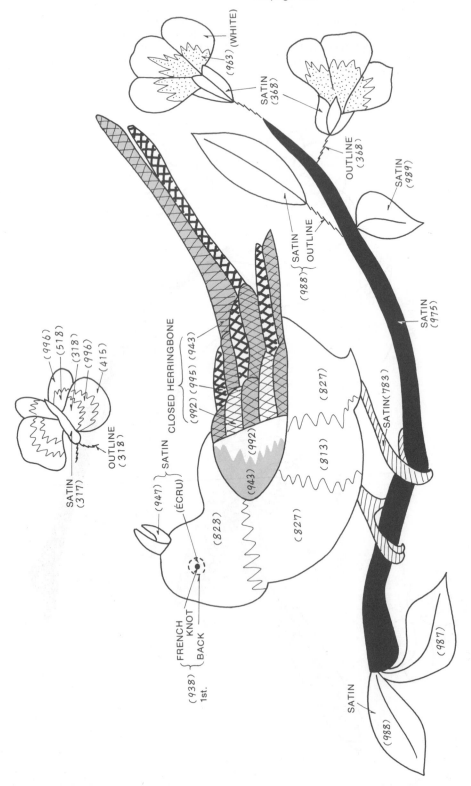

shown on page 39, top

MATERIALS

Fabric: Navy blue linen, 30 cm by 25 cm.

Threads: D.M.C. #25 six-strand embroidery floss. 1 skein each of 318, 415 (ash grey), 435 (umber) and 469 (moss green). ½ skein each of 304 (scarlet), 349, 350, 351 (geranium red), 760 (morocco red) and 936 (moss green). Small amount each of 317, 414 (ash grey), 725, 726 (saffron), 782, 783 (golden yellow), 938 (coffee brown), 943 (jade green) and écru.

Frame, 24.5 cm by 19.5 cm (inside measurement).

FINISHED SIZE: Same size as frame.

DIRECTIONS: Work in same manner as indicated on page 131.

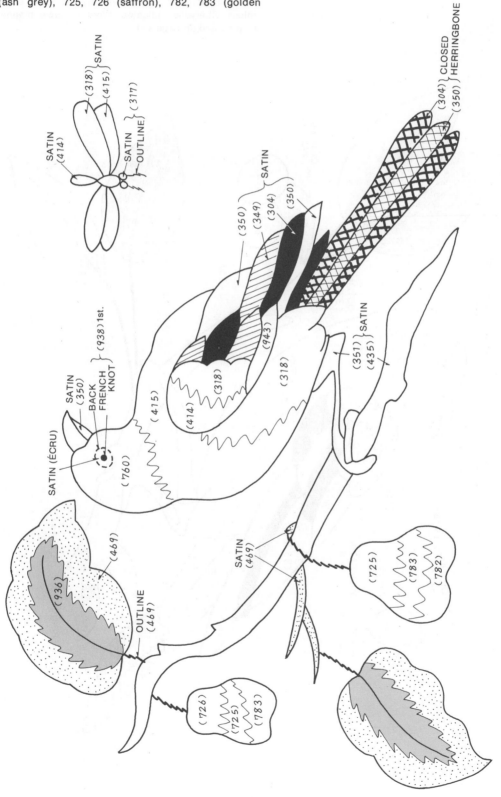

shown on page 39, bottom

MATERIALS

Fabric: Navy blue linen, 30 cm by 25 cm.

Threads: D.M.C. #25 six-strand embroidery floss. 1 skein of 435 (umber). ½ skein each of 347 (cardinal red), 676, 677 (old gold), 977 (umber gold), 3045, 3046, 3047 (beige), 3328 (morocco red), 3345, 3346, 3347 (scarab green) and écru. Small amount each of 415 (ash grey), 606, 608 (flame red), 632 (chocolate), 680, 729 (old gold), 938 (coffee brown), 971 (canary yellow), 975 (umber gold) and 3348 (scarab green).

Frame, 24.5 cm by 19.5 cm (inside measurement).

FINISHED SIZE: Same size as frame.

DIRECTION: Work all embroidery in satin stitch unless otherwise indicated. Work in same manner as indicated on page 131.

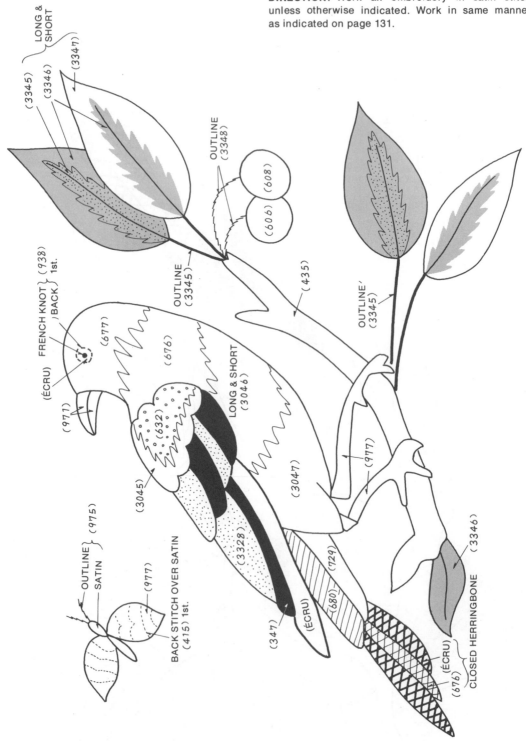

134

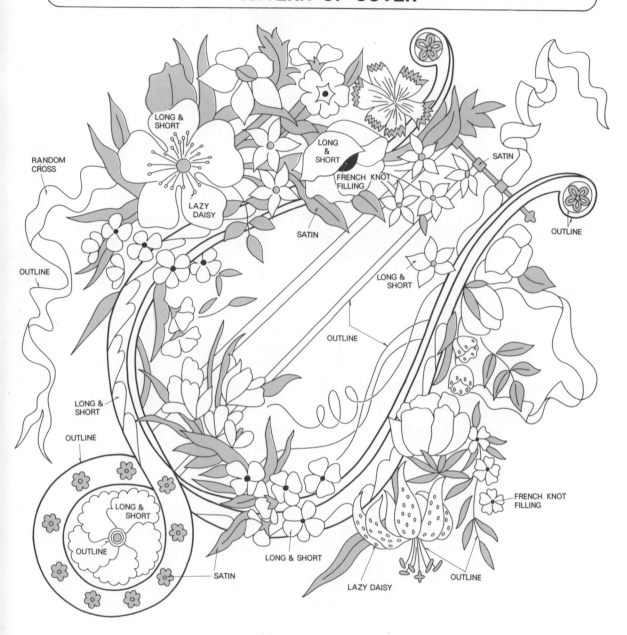